Backwards Planning

Author
Harriet Isecke

Foreword by
Wendy Conklin

SHELL EDUCATION

Publishing Credits

Dona Herweck Rice, *Editor-in-Chief*; Lee Aucoin, *Creative Director*;
Don Tran, *Print Production Manager;* Lori Kamola, M.S.Ed., *Editorial Director*;
Sara Johnson, *Senior Editor;* Hillary Wolfe, *Editor*; Juan Chavolla, *Cover/Interior Layout Designer;*
Corinne Burton, M.A.Ed., *Publisher*

Shell Educational Publishing

5301 Oceanus Drive
Huntington Beach, CA 92649-1030
www.shelleducation.com

ISBN 978-1-4258-0633-0

© 2011 Shell Educational Publishing, Inc.

Table of Contents

Foreword

If only we could just know the future before living it, then we would avoid so many mistakes. We could chart our paths better and make strong purposeful decisions. Say goodbye to wasted time and needless worry! If only ...

While this wishful thinking is not possible when it comes to living our lives, it can be very useful when applied to curriculum design. Most curriculum professionals at the district levels look at their maps (standards) and begin charting paths for their teachers to teach those standards. First you teach this, then you teach that, then you teach the next thing until the standards are decisively met. It is very similar to going on a trip with a destination in mind. Rarely does one go on a long road trip without mapping out a path. People who like to be extra prepared decide what towns they will stop in to eat, shop, and use the facilities. They take out those old road maps from Rand McNally or just download the latest GPS phone app. Just like the standards, these helpful tools guide people to their desired destinations.

But, what if we took a different approach as it applies to curriculum design? What if we started with the standard, objective, or the big idea and then worked our way backwards step-by-step? We could develop strategic formative assessments based on the end summative assessment. We could build in time for re-teaching. Chances are, we would eliminate useless steps and missteps. With the objective, standard, or big idea as the goal, we would carefully plan for all students to reach that standard through purposeful differentiation. No longer would our differentiation merely consist of hope that some day the students will reach the goal. The scaffolded assignments would be geared so that the students would grow incrementally in their understanding. Every ounce of energy would drive towards that end goal.

Backwards planning enables differentiation to be most effective. All of us are guilty at one time or another of just differentiating without really thinking of the ultimate goal. Sure, we want our students to learn and grow, and that's why we differentiate assignments. But sometimes, we differentiate assignments only to meet the needs of our diverse learners in that one lesson without thinking of how we will get them to the ultimate goal of learning the objective. This type of differentiation is more like a crutch than an avenue. Differentiation is most effective when it is two fold: meeting our students where they are at and moving them towards the finish line of learning the objectives. Backwards planning and differentiation combine the best of both worlds.

During my first few years in the classroom, I wish I had had the foresight to know that planning with the end in mind is a more efficient way of teaching. I was only worried about getting through the dense curriculum by year's end. My colleagues were on that racetrack, too. Instead of professional learning communities, we worked independently. No one was there to help us troubleshoot problems, to challenge our understanding of learning, to collaborate on the best teaching strategies, and to support us when we tried to change for the betterment of our students. Backwards planning is the key that synthesizes all the important things we know about teaching. It encourages collaboration, purposeful differentiation, and the best teaching strategies. Backwards planning is the road map to producing successful students. And that produces a very rewarding by-product…knowing you've succeeded as a teacher.

—Wendy Conklin, M.A.

The Foundations of Great Teaching

Calvin Coolidge once said, "It is easy to do the right thing. The hard part is knowing what the right thing is." This thought has always touched me. I feel strongly that true happiness comes from finding the right thing to do with your life and then dedicating yourself to it; but recognizing the "right thing" didn't come easily to me.

When I finished college at the University of Michigan, I wasn't certain about what I wanted to do. I heard that New York City was desperately looking for teachers, and that any college graduate willing to take a free summer course could get emergency certification and be guaranteed a job for a year. This seemed like a good idea at the time. So, after eight weeks of coursework and a full 20 minutes of student teaching, I was actually deemed adequately prepared for the classroom by the state of New York and put in charge of my very first class of 30 rambunctious youngsters. I loved those students and wanted desperately to help them. The problem was that I had no idea what to do with them, and I didn't know where to turn for help. When I got up my nerve and asked a few colleagues for suggestions during lunch, they told me that they didn't want to discuss students during their free time. That fall, I took my last required course entitled Problems in the Classroom. I remember the professor asking us what was our most pressing problem. I raised my hand and sadly admitted, "I don't know what to do between 9:00 A.M. and 3:00 P.M.."

Learning how to be an effective teacher became my life's mission, and I decided that if I ever mastered it, I would help anyone else who asked. No one should ever have to feel as alone and discouraged as I did that first year.

I've become convinced over my many years as a classroom teacher, graduate student, instructional coach, school administrator, author, and educational consultant, that great teaching stems from a deep passion to help children become all that they can be. I can't think of any work that touches the future more than teaching. Great teaching helps children form deep and enduring understandings about the world in which they live, and it turns them into explorers, thinkers, discoverers, imaginers, and wonderers. But being a great teacher is obviously easier said than done. Great teachers care about their students, and they work hard to do their best every day. However, passion alone isn't enough. There are some vital prerequisites that must be in place in order to be effective.

To Become a Great Teacher You Must...

Know your subject. It stands to reason that you cannot teach something you don't know. This sounds simple, but unfortunately, it is not always the case. Sometimes teachers are given assignments that are not in their field of expertise. Here is a sad example: Early in my teaching career, the science specialist in my school came running to me before class. She quickly asked, "Does the sun revolve around Earth, or does Earth revolve around the sun? I'm teaching this next period and I forget!" The school made a poor decision in hiring this person for the science position, but the teacher didn't help the situation either. She didn't take any responsibility in actually learning the material before she taught it. I shudder to think what the students learned in science that year!

Have knowledge about what it takes to teach your specific content or topic. Being knowledgeable about content alone isn't enough. (Just think back to some of your college professors!) Some experts find the information in their fields so obvious that they are unable to distinguish between what is easy and what is difficult for others to learn. And just because someone is an expert doesn't mean that he or she can give clear explanations. A teacher must know the foundational knowledge and skills that students need in order to understand the central concepts of their subjects or topics, and must be able to tap into their students' relevant prior knowledge to help them make the necessary connections. A teacher must also figure out the typical difficulties that students might encounter as they learn new material, and determine which strategies are the most helpful in assisting students who struggle. This takes time and careful observation to learn. A new teacher may wish to ask an effective and experienced teacher for assistance in understanding the materials with which students are most likely to struggle, and for the most effective ways to approach difficult topics. Schools should facilitate this type of idea exchange in their mentorship programs.

Know classroom management techniques. If you can't get (and keep) your students' attention, it doesn't matter how well informed you are about your subject or about good instruction. Students cannot learn in an atmosphere that is disorganized, chaotic, or dangerous. In his book, *The First Days of School: How to Be an Effective Teacher* (1998; 2001), Harry Wong, a guru of classroom management, clearly outlines effective management techniques and explains a common mistake that many inexperienced teachers make in confusing rules with procedures. According to Wong, rules govern behavioral expectations, while procedures govern how things are done. Teachers should set only a few meaningful rules, and consequences for breaking these rules should be clear, fair, consistent, and practical. Rules should be expressed in positive ways such as "do your own work" or "respect your own and other people's property." Teachers can reinforce rules by referring to them when they are being followed, not just when they are being broken.

Procedures on the other hand, are the "how-tos" of the classroom. They are the processes students need to follow so that the room operates smoothly. Procedures include what you want your students to do in different circumstances, such as when they enter or leave the room; when you signal for their attention; when materials need to be distributed or collected; when they work with partners or in groups; when they need to sharpen a pencil; and when they need to use materials and resources that are not at their desks. Procedures need to be explained and demonstrated carefully. According to Wong (1998; 2001), you do not punish students when they fail to follow procedures correctly. You just have students rehearse the procedures repeatedly until they become routine. Your procedures need to be well thought-out, consistent, clear, efficient, and very well-practiced.

Assess the needs of your students on an ongoing basis, and adjust your teaching based on what you discover. Giving tests just for the sake of collecting grades isn't appropriate. Most of the assessments you give should be formative, or used to inform or modify your instruction. You need to give assessments to find out what your students know and what confusions they have while you teach. This way, you can determine what to teach next and how to do it effectively.

Of course, you'll need to analyze assessment results quickly in order to tailor your instruction to the current needs of your students. Not all assessments need to be written; some should be performance-based so that you can see how well your students can apply what they are learning. This might mean that your students present information, participate in a debate or performance, discuss their research, create and explain an original project or invention, perform and analyze an experiment, or explain how they solved a problem, and so on.

Part of assessment involves becoming a keen student observer. Students reveal what they know and are ready to learn in many ways, both directly and indirectly. By carefully examining their actions, questions, answers, and conversations, you can see what your students already understand as well as the misconceptions they may have. By listening to students and looking at the work they produce, you can see what skills they possess, what they are confident about accomplishing, where they worry they might fail, what they enjoy, and what they dislike. What your students reveal to you about their skills, their interests, and their learning styles will help you continually target instruction to students' needs in both formal and informal ways. Although this may seem challenging at first, it will soon become second nature and will help you become a great teacher!

Understand effective instructional techniques. One of the fundamental techniques used in teaching is the Gradual Release of Responsibility Model. This comes from the work of Pearson and Gallagher (1983). In this model, the teacher begins by modeling the new learning, guiding students carefully through it to make sure that they understand what they are doing, and then gradually releasing the responsibility of learning to them. Students need lots of time to construct meaning through independent practice and problem solving as they use new concepts and skills. (See Appendix A on pages 159–160 for a more in-depth look at this model.)

One More Prerequisite

Keep your goals clearly in mind as you plan. The main goal of teaching is to help students gain an enduring understanding of the important ideas behind the topics which they are studying. To help your students do this, you need to design your lessons around the results that you want your students to achieve and the *big ideas* you want them to fully understand. An effective method for creating consistently good, useful units of study is called Backwards Planning, which is based on *Understanding by Design* (UbD). This method was originally developed by Grant Wiggins and Jay McTighe, and detailed in their book with this title in 1998. Backwards Planning is the major topic of this book.

I will not pretend that this type of thoughtful planning is easy, but I can assure you that it is worth the effort, and this book offers plenty of guidance, suggestions, and examples to help you along the way.

An Overview of This Book

The essential question that this book addresses is how to design units of study and lessons so that students achieve enduring understanding. When you teach for enduring understanding, your students do not simply memorize isolated facts, which may seem pointless to them; rather, they mull over interesting big ideas and construct their own meanings about the underlying concepts that define a topic. Students learn how to apply their knowledge in new situations and use what they know to solve real problems.

However, one looming question remains: How can this be accomplished in a way that is manageable? Lofty ideals are great, but it is important to be practical. Professor Seymour Papert from MIT (2009) rightly pointed out that teachers cannot just be preoccupied with what they could do someday. They need to know what they can do on Monday.

Let's face it—teaching is a highly stressful job. Teachers are responsible for what students in their classrooms learn on a daily basis. But that's not all. Teachers also share responsibility for the motivation, the emotional well-being, and the confidence of the children they serve, and they must answer to administrators and parents, as well as to students. Teachers are very busy people, and one thing is certain: They are never given enough planning time. Teaching for enduring understanding is a great idea, and like other great ideas, it can lead to great results. However, this type of teaching takes time and effort to learn.

As Albert Einstein once said, "Any intelligent fool can make things bigger, more complex.... It takes a touch of genius—and a lot of courage—to move in the opposite direction. Everything should be made as simple as possible, but not simpler." The purpose of this book is to demystify the planning process. It is to show educators how to plan for students' enduring understanding in the simplest, most practical way possible without watering down the richness of the process. In this book, we explore both the reasons for teaching for enduring understanding, and the specific procedures for making this type of planning as simple, effective, and efficient as possible.

This book progresses through three main ideas: The rationale and research behind Backwards Planning, how to use Backwards Planning to design a unit of instruction, and how to keep differentiated instruction and classroom management at the heart of lesson design.

Chapter 1 discusses the basic components and principles of Understanding by Design (or Backwards Planning).

Chapter 2 examines what "understanding" actually means, how students construct meaning, and different ways that students can demonstrate depth of understanding. This chapter also introduces six facets of learning that should be taken into consideration while planning.

Chapter 3 discusses the tradeoffs between breadth vs. depth instruction and deals with how to decide which topics lend themselves to in depth study. This chapter also details different ways to design units of study using Understanding by Design principles.

Chapter 4 addresses Stage One of Backwards Planning. It explains how to determine the goals of your unit of study. It deals with using standards, determining the big ideas, writing essential (or guiding) questions, establishing learning targets, and developing exciting and authentic culminating projects. This chapter also features an ecology unit that you can use as a model for your own planning.

Chapter 5 addresses Stage Two of Backwards Planning. It examines different types of formal and informal assessments that give you the information you need to teach effectively.

Chapter 6 focuses on selecting or creating assessments and rubrics that promote student understanding. It describes a format for peer feedback groups that will help your students work constructively with one another, and it describes ways that you can respond to your students to optimize their achievement.

Chapter 7 deals with Stage Three of the Backwards Planning process. It is filled with ideas about how to plan effective and engaging daily lesson activities. It gives you step-by-step techniques that will help your students master information, apply what they know to create something original, and solve novel problems.

Chapter 8 deals with the paradigm shift that schools face in preparing students for the global challenges of the future. It explores the need for instruction targeted toward students' needs, interests, and learning styles, and shows how differentiated instruction can be tied to the Backwards Planning model. This section gives specific ideas on how to effectively differentiate instruction through content, process, and product.

Chapter 9 explores ways to organize and manage a student-centered classroom, including ideas for room set-up, establishing procedures for group work, and efficient record-keeping techniques.

Several Appendices contain templates, planning tools, and lesson ideas to help you as you begin your own journey through Backwards Planning.

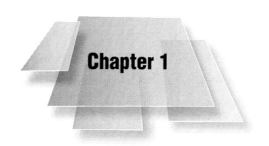

Chapter 1

The Big Ideas Behind Backwards Planning

I was considered to be an excellent student when I was in school. Driven by my desire for approval, I pleased my teachers, paid attention, handed in assignments on time, and followed all of the rules. I memorized whatever was asked of me for quizzes and tests. I didn't ask many questions, but I knew how to play the game; I could get good grades even when the material was uninteresting or made little or no sense to me. However, it's very telling that even though I did very well, I remember little of what I learned. My husband, on the other hand, was a terrible student. He has always been a naturally inquisitive person with a deep passion for making sense of the world around him. To this day, he is constantly trying to use what he knows to solve new problems. However, when he was in school he apparently had no interest in pleasing his teachers and found his classes both irrelevant and boring. He got away with doing as little schoolwork as possible. What he did do was to personally challenge himself by trying to read an entire book under his desk every day. Just like me, my husband remembers very little from school, but because he was driven by his desire to make sense of the world around him, and not by his desire to get approval, he built up a deep and enduring framework of understanding about many different subjects. To this day, I still tease him about his lousy grades!

William Lowe Bryan once said, "Education is one of the few things a person is willing to pay for and not get." Over the years, I have thought long and hard about the different ways in which my husband and I approached school. It has become obvious to me that ownership is essential to learning. You cannot force any type of meaningful understanding upon another person. Learners have to actively make sense of the world around them in order to end up with any lasting understanding. This realization had huge implications for me as a teacher. I wanted to make sure that the education I provided for my students amounted to more than just an arbitrary list of things they felt they needed to do to please me or to get good grades. I needed to get real student buy-in. I knew that my instruction had to have direction, organization, coherence, and, above all, clear purpose in order for my students to ultimately become eager and active participants in their own learning. I had to pique their curiosity and put their interests and needs squarely at the center of instruction.

There was much that I needed to think about to make this happen. First, I had to determine my long-term goals. I had to think beyond the day-to-day planning and identify what I wanted my students to carry with them long after they left my classroom. Even before I had the words to express the idea properly, I understood that I had to teach for enduring understanding to be able to make the most important difference that I could in the lives of my students. These enduring understandings would be the true benefits that my students would gain from having me as their teacher. And I realized that I needed to both clearly identify what I wanted the results of my teaching to be, and determine how I could get my students to deeply explore the central concepts I was teaching *before* I could plan my lessons effectively. This meant planning using a backwards design model.

Research That Supports Backwards Planning

The *Understanding by Design* framework by Wiggins and McTighe (1998) is rooted in 30 years of cognitive psychology research. A summary of that research can be found in the book, *How People Learn: Brain, Mind, Experience, and School* (Bransford, Brown, and Cocking 1999). Psychologists, neuroscientists, and educators have examined the conditions necessary for people to gain deep understanding and apply what they have learned to new situations. The results of the research clearly show that enduring understanding cannot be guided by rote memory. A learner must explore the underlying concepts and principles behind the facts in order to form a deep and lasting understanding of any subject.

In the earlier part of the twentieth century, the demands of the workplace were fairly straightforward. Most education focused on the acquisition of reading, writing, and calculating skills. Students needed to memorize basic facts and figures and learn important biblical and literary passages. Schools did not train students to think critically or imaginatively, to express themselves persuasively, to apply their knowledge to solve novel problems, or to develop their own creative solutions. People who were considered highly educated at that time were knowledgeable about history, geography, mathematics, Latin, and religion, and could recite long passages from the great classics of literature.

The last several decades have brought dramatic global changes. These changes have had tremendous consequences, and have revolutionized the demands that we now must place on our schools. Huge amounts of information (and misinformation) are literally at people's fingertips because of technology. The sheer magnitude of accessible human knowledge is expanding at such a rapid rate that schools cannot hope to cover even a small fraction of what is needed. The new pressures of the workplace require people to recognize which information is reliable and relevant, to collaborate with each other, and to think productively. It is no longer enough to simply remember and repeat information. Thus, the very definition of effective learning in schools has shifted from a model that once emphasized drill, practice, and recall to one whose goal has become "the understanding and application of knowledge" (Bransford, Brown, and Cocking 1999).

The last several decades have also brought about significant brain research. Cognitive researchers have examined what constitutes expertise in different subject areas. The idea is that experts are people who are able to make the best use of their knowledge, so we should teach our students to think like experts. Studies revealed several defining characteristics that distinguish experts from novices. Important differences were found in how experts and novices organize and store information, and in how they approach new problems. These differences have important implications for effective learning.

What are the basic differences between how experts and novices store, organize, and retrieve information? Expert knowledge does not simply consist of discrete facts or procedures. Instead, experts organize what they know around their subject's core concepts or big ideas. In other words, experts have a framework of big ideas that they clearly understand and can use. They fit new relevant information into that framework so that they can easily retrieve it. Novices, on the other hand, might be able to recall some basic facts or figures about a topic, but may have difficulty seeing the greater relevance of the information, or retrieving it when needed.

What are the specific differences between how experts and novices approach new problems? Experts in all fields first attempt to understand a new problem before they try to solve it. When faced with a new problem, experts mull over its important implications. Since their knowledge is organized into meaningful patterns of information that support understanding and transfer rather than only the ability to remember, they can both retrieve the information they need efficiently and transfer or apply it to come up with an accurate solution. In contrast, novices are more likely to jump in and attempt to solve a new problem quickly, without necessarily understanding it. Since their information is not highly organized, novices may not know what is relevant, and therefore are more likely to immediately seek correct formulas or pat answers.

It follows that if our goal as teachers is to enable our students to apply their learning to solve new problems, we need to help them organize information into meaningful patterns, just as experts do. We can no longer teach skills and knowledge in an isolated or narrow context. Transfer only becomes possible when the learner understands the guiding principles behind the facts and formulas. Unfortunately, the transfer of knowledge doesn't always come easily to students. We can speed the process by showing our students the relevance of what they are learning. We need to give them specifics about when, where, what, and how the things that they are learning can be used. We also need to provide them with plenty of time to practice applying what they learn in new circumstances.

Before we examine how the human brain receives, stores, and retrieves information and what the term *understanding* actually means, let us take a closer look at the specific features of the planning process that Grant Wiggins and Jay McTighe called Understanding by Design (1998).

What Is Understanding by Design?

Understanding by Design (UbD, or Backwards Planning) is a specific process for planning units of study. You begin by deciding what you want the final results of your instruction to be, and then you plan "backwards" to figure out how to get there. Grant Wiggins and Jay McTighe introduced Understanding by Design in 1998 in their book of that title. As they explain, Backwards Planning, or planning with the end in mind, is not really backwards in actuality. For example, when you plan a vacation, you determine what kind of vacation you want and where you will go before you decide how you will get there and exactly what you will pack. But Backwards Planning is different from the way that many teachers traditionally prepare lessons and deliver instruction. Many teachers become so bogged down by day-to-day survival that they do not think in terms of the final result. Some may follow a teacher's guide from beginning to end, or provide disconnected or loosely connected activities for students to keep them busy. Some try to cover an entire textbook (or body of knowledge) without a clear, long-term goal in mind. Many teachers go right to their daily lessons without thinking about the deep and enduring understandings that they want their students to have as a result of their instruction.

Understanding by Design is not a pre-packaged educational program with a specified scope and sequence. The idea behind it is that teachers are professionals who need to have control over what they teach. Teachers can decide how to design units of instruction that promote understanding by using what Wiggins and Grant term specific design principles. This is one of the ideas that we explore in great depth throughout this book.

In both their original book and in their newer *Understanding by Design Expanded 2nd Edition* (2005, 22), Wiggins and McTighe provide a useful UbD planning template that presents an overview of the three stages of UbD:

Stage One: Identify Desired Results

Stage Two: Determine the Assessment Evidence

Stage Three: Plan Learning Experiences and Instruction

Stage One: Identify Desired Results

In Stage One of Backwards Planning, we start by identifying the big ideas and guiding principles that we want our students to use as the organizing structure for learning. We specify exactly what we want our students to know and be able to do, and we figure out how we can help them organize what they learn to solve new problems. We then need to plan backwards to create a road map for instruction that will lead our students from where they are to where we want them to be.

Research reveals that covering many topics in a superficial way does not help students to develop the skills they need. In fact, covering too much content could lead to the development of disconnected rather than connected knowledge. It might actually prevent students from organizing what they know because they don't have enough time to learn it in sufficient depth.

Curricula, therefore, should emphasize depth over breadth of knowledge. In creating units of study using Backwards Planning, it is not possible to teach everything. You need to prioritize and determine what is worthy of enduring understanding, which aspects of your instruction require in-depth exploration, and what information to skip.

Effective instruction also requires the teacher to assess student knowledge on a continual basis. Assessments must match the learning goals if they are to be effective. If the goal is to foster deep understanding and transfer, it is not enough to give assessments that mainly focus on recalling facts and formulas. This type of information is quickly forgotten because it is not used regularly, and it does not lead to a conceptual understanding of underlying principles.

Stage Two: Determine the Assessment Evidence

Students must be required to explain and demonstrate that they know when, where, why, and how to use their knowledge. Thus, Stage Two of Backwards Planning requires that you determine which types of assessments will give you the most useful information about what your students know and are able to do. The most useful assessments will help you pinpoint any confusion that your students have. You then need to use this information to target your instruction toward meeting their changing needs.

The research also shows that students need timely and specific feedback to learn efficiently and effectively. Some teachers give too little feedback, feedback that is too general, or feedback that is offered too late for students to revise what they are thinking or doing. Teachers need to clarify students' confusions while they are in the process of learning. This gives the students a chance to improve the quality of their thinking and understanding, and helps them make meaningful improvements to their work. Most assessments in school are summative and occur at the end of an assignment or project. Summative feedback, especially when delayed, may be good for grading students, but is basically useless in the learning process.

Stage Three: Plan Learning Experiences and Instruction

Research reveals that different disciplines of study are organized in different ways. Disciplines have their own specific methods of inquiry and different requirements for what constitutes evidence. For example, the evidence that proves a historical claim is different from the evidence needed to support a scientific hypothesis. It is *not* true that a good teacher can teach any subject with equal levels of effectiveness. Teachers need to have specific pedagogical content knowledge to be effective in their respective disciplines, but content knowledge alone is insufficient for effective teaching. Teachers must know which instructional methods will likely engage students and help them understand the specific content that is being taught.

Thus, in Stage Three of Backwards Planning, you figure out the optimal way to structure lessons for your particular discipline so that your students can achieve the goals of the unit. You need to set up your classroom so that your students construct meaning about the big ideas of your topic or subject from the work that they do. Students need to be actively engaged in thought, work, and continual reflection. They cannot sit back and be passive recipients of your valuable knowledge.

Remember that in order to remain motivated, students must feel that the work that they do is useful, relevant, and authentic. Authentic assignments require high-level thinking and have value beyond the classroom. If students fail to see the value or relevance in what they are doing, they probably will not be inspired to put in the effort to make deep connections. Meaningful learning takes place when students work on things that they know have real value. That is when they will reach the enduring understandings that they can apply in the real world.

Backwards Planning Overview

This book expands on the original Understanding by Design process and focuses on how the brain deals with information and constructs meaning. It explains specific brain-friendly strategies that you can use to teach for enduring understanding and also has many concrete classroom examples to help guide you through both the planning and implementation processes. However, before we go in depth, the chart on pages 26–27 gives a very simple overview of the elements of each stage of Backwards Planning. If this is your first brush with UbD, or if you want to see examples of the types of questions to ask, you will find Appendix B (pages 161–162) to be very useful in providing an "at-a-glance" look at this model, and Appendix C (page 163) offers a simple planning template to help you get started.

Simple Overview of Backwards Planning Principles

Stage One: Identify Desired Results

What should my students know, understand, and be able to do? What is worthy of understanding? What enduring understandings are desired? (Wiggins and McTighe 1998). What are the goals at the heart of your unit of study? The following design principles will help you identify your end results:

Determine the Content Standard(s) (Established Goals)

- What are the standards (local, state, national) for the coursework you are teaching?
- What are students expected to learn?

Determine the Big Idea(s) or Enduring Understanding(s)

- What are the big ideas (universal concepts that have enduring relevance) at the heart of the subject or topic which you are teaching?
- What are the likely misunderstandings that need to be addressed?

Determine the Essential or Guiding Question(s)

- What open-ended, thought-provoking questions will foster disciplined inquiry and investigation?
- What questions will call upon students to examine their own experiences and content knowledge?
- What questions will help students use and build knowledge effectively over time?

Determine the Student Objectives

- What observable and measurable outcomes can you assess?

Determine the Knowledge Learning Targets

- What facts, concepts, and principles do students need to learn in order to reach the goals?

Determine the Procedural Learning Targets

- What procedures, strategies, methods, and skills will students be able to use as a result of this unit of study?

Design the Culminating Activity

- How will students demonstrate that they really understand and can apply the big ideas of the unit of study (e.g., projects, presentations, performance assessments, assignments, or tasks)?
- How can this culminating experience be authentic so that it has relevance beyond the classroom?

Simple Overview of Backwards Planning Principles *(cont.)*

Stage Two: Determine the Assessment Evidence

In this stage you determine what your students must do to prove that they are meeting the learning goals of the unit of study. How will you know that your students are truly "getting" what you are teaching and not just parroting what is being taught?

- What types of assessments will give you the most information about how well your students are doing? What kinds will pinpoint their confusions?

- What types of assessments will show you whether or not your students can transfer their knowledge and apply it to new situations?

- What anecdotal evidence will you use to determine how well your students are achieving?

- What criteria will you use to judge student progress?

- How can you use what you learn about your students to inform your daily instruction? How will you help students who struggle or who exceed expectations?

- How will you have students assess themselves and reflect on their learning?

Stage Three: Plan Learning Experiences and Instruction

In this stage you plan out your daily lessons and activities. Your unit must contain the pertinent information from the curriculum that will foster the enduring understandings that you want your students to acquire. Think about how to engage your students in meaningful and authentic learning experiences that will help them reach the goals of instruction. In other words, you need to plan motivating day-to-day lessons and activities that will result in the understandings, skills, and knowledge outlined in Stage One.

- Which concepts will take the most time to teach?

- How will assignments help students construct meaning?

- Which skills require direct instruction? Which skills should be taught through student investigation?

- How will students apply their knowledge?

- What are some ways students can reflect on their progress?

- What materials will be required?

- How will instruction be differentiated?

Conclusion

To teach students to understand, retrieve, and use information like experts, you need to organize and structure their learning around the big ideas of the topics that you are teaching. Students need to study important topics in sufficient depth to make meaningful connections. They need to understand when, where, and how to use what they are learning to solve new problems and practice new skills in different contexts. Teachers must plan engaging daily lessons that are organized around central concepts. Teachers should continually assess student understanding and target instruction appropriately. Finally, students need ongoing, constructive feedback to raise their level of understanding and to improve their quality of thought and work. They need to reflect on their progress and take ownership of their learning. The time and effort it will take to plan for enduring understanding will be rewarded with student enthusiasm, involvement, and lifetime achievement.

Reflection

1. What are three or four "big ideas" at the heart of a subject or topic that you teach? How can first determining the "big ideas" help you plan your instruction for enduring understanding?

2. How can you use assessments to help focus instruction and make it more effective?

3. How can you ensure that the "big ideas" of your topic or subject are reinforced in your assignments?

4. How can you make your assignments relevant and authentic?

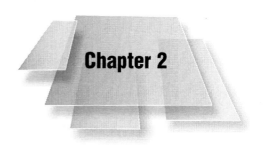

Chapter 2

The Principles of Backwards Planning

In thinking about the purpose of Backwards Planning, it may be helpful to think of a real-life example. Let's consider an all-too-familiar scenario: It's New Year's Eve, and for the umpteenth time you have made a resolution to lose weight, eat well, and get healthy. You're going to try to live a longer and healthier life. (We might even call this the ultimate "enduring principle!") On January 1, you sign up for the local gym, head to the supermarket and purchase salads, a slew of vitamins and supplements, and a few foods with strange combined misspellings of words, such as soybacon-tofurkey cheeseburger. By February 12, you've become too busy to go to the gym, your fat-free, sugar-free, flavor-free ice cream is mocking you from the freezer, and your old jeans are still too tight. You haven't taken your vitamins in two weeks, you are stressed at work, and all you crave is one measly deep-dish pizza dripping with melted cheese. Just one pizza couldn't hurt, right? So you pick up the phone, and well, let's face it, we all know how it goes from there.

So, what's the problem here? Without a roadmap to follow, the entire process becomes too difficult; and without achievable benchmarks along the way, you feel unrewarded by your early efforts. Your original goals are vague, and you had no concrete plan to get there, so when faced with real-life problems, you just give up. Oh well. Maybe you don't have to think about this again until the summer bathing suit panic. Or, just maybe, there is a better way.

The Nature of Understanding

Now, go through this same resolution but apply Backwards Planning. You begin by identifying your desired result: living a long and healthy life. (This is the only part that parallels the last example.) Examine some understandings at the heart of your goal, essential questions you would need to answer to meet it, and the things you would need to know and do to reach it.

First, look at the enduring understanding around the idea of a healthy life. The "big idea" might be that maintaining this long-term life goal requires a long-term change in lifestyle, not just a temporary fix. And the understandings you need are both factual and metacognitive. First, you need to understand the elements of a healthful lifestyle. Then, you need to think about your own values. You need to understand what you could easily change about the way you live, what would be more difficult to change (but still manageable), and what you would never change (and why). You would then consider some essential or guiding questions:

- What do I need to do to reach my goal?

- How do I get to the optimum weight range for my height and build, and how do I maintain it?

- What physical exercise do I need to do to get in shape and stay that way, and how could that be accomplished?

- How can I protect myself from getting sick? What can I do to avoid stress and to promote my emotional well-being?

You must figure out the specific knowledge and skill sets that are necessary to accomplish your goal. (These are your learning targets.) You would have to know what foods (and the proper amounts) that are nutritious for you. You would need to know about your body, the types of exercises you need to get and stay in shape, and how to do these exercises. You would need to know how much rest you need to get, and how to protect yourself from contagious diseases. In terms of skills, you would have to be able to plan and prepare wholesome meals, exercise in varied and suitable ways, take appropriate precautions against diseases, and so on.

Next, you need to figure out how you will know if you are headed in the right direction. (This is your assessment evidence). Your end goal may be far off. You need to set benchmarks or specific ways of marking your progress along the way. Perhaps you could set a weekly weight loss goal, an exercise goal, or an activity goal. You might think about the adjustments you might make if you find yourself falling behind (or exceeding) the benchmarks you've set. This will prevent you from getting so discouraged that you quit, or so overly confident that you lose sight of what you are doing.

Finally, you would plan your daily schedule of meals, exercise, and activities based on your desired results. This is your learning plan, where you organize your time so that you can fit in the things that are emotionally, physically, psychologically, and socially important for your health and well-being.

You have to be thoughtful and flexible throughout the process. Life is unpredictable, so you need to be aware of how you are doing and be able to respond to whatever happens. Remember, you are in this for the long haul, so you must continually remain flexible so that you can make allowances for things that you cannot foresee. But even as you remain flexible and make the necessary adjustments, you will always need to keep your end goal firmly in mind.

Think about the benefits of this approach. You have a goal and you have a workable plan for reaching it. You can mark your progress as you proceed, and you can flexibly make adjustments when you see what is working well and what isn't. In the end, if you adjust your plans as necessary, and stick to working towards your final goal, you will have the best chance of achieving what you set out to achieve. The best part about this is that with all of your good habits, you'll probably have a long life, and will be able to torture yourself with lots of different New Year's resolutions in the future!

The same principles that apply to the weight loss example also apply to teaching. As educators, we need to think about our goals. We need to determine exactly what is worthy of enduring understanding. If we don't know where we want our students to end up, we cannot effectively plan how to help them get there. We need to be specific about what we want our students to learn and be able to do as a result of our instruction. Without benchmarks to reach, and effective ways to measure progress along the way, we will not be able to target our instruction appropriately. If we do not plan our day-to-day activities with our students' needs in mind, the lessons we deliver and the results we get will be haphazard at best.

The concept of understanding is a complex one. When students understand, they make connections in their brains. Since it happens internally, it is something for which we need evidence after the fact.

Knowledge and understanding are both central to learning, but they are not the same thing. In order to teach for enduring understanding, we need to distinguish between knowledge and understanding. For example, students can have knowledge of the names and dates of different historical events. They may even memorize their major causes and effects, but doing so does not give them meaningful insight into the significance of these events. They may not understand how people's lives could have been altered if the historical events had resulted in different outcomes. They may not make any connections between historical events and current events, and therefore may not understand how we might change present actions to prevent possibly negative future outcomes. What we learn from history is vitally important. As British statesman and philosopher Edmund Burke (1729–1797) wisely stated, "Those who don't know history are destined to repeat it." (But it is important to know the facts, too! As my college history professor used to say, "Those who don't know history will repeat it next semester.")

Understanding is the awareness of the connection between different pieces of information. Understanding implies that a person can appropriately use what he or she knows in different circumstances.

In their book, *Understanding by Design* (1998), Grant Wiggins and Jay McTighe present six ways in which students can demonstrate their understanding of what they are learning. They call these "Facets of Understanding." They are as follows:

- The student has the ability to explain.
- The student has the ability to interpret.
- The student has the ability to apply.
- The student has gained new perspectives.
- The student has the ability to empathize.
- The student has self-knowledge.

The chart on pages 34–36 gives an overview of these six facets. It includes questions that teachers may ask to elicit evidence of each type of understanding, and ways that students can respond successfully. Remember, there is more than one way for students to show that they understand. Understanding can be demonstrated by talking, by writing, through experiments, debates, artwork, performances, and so on.

The Six Facets of Understanding

Facets of Understanding	Tasks and Questions for Students
Facet 1: The student has the ability to explain The student clearly tells or shows how something works, what happened and why, or how the idea fits into a broader context.	• State a clear, complete, justified account of what was learned in your own words. • How would you explain this idea to a small child? An expert in the field? A person with the opposite view? A person with only two minutes to listen? A person whose life depends upon knowing this concept? • How can you justify your position? What proof do you have? • What are the implications? • How do you know this is true? • What connections can you make between this and other things that you have learned?
Facet 2: The student has the ability to interpret The student tells relevant stories that bring new light to what he or she has learned.	• Give a meaningful narrative, translation, or personal story that clarifies or extends the meaning of the concept. • What significance does this have? • When has this concept mattered in our lives? Why? • How can this idea be extended? • What might likely happen if this idea is repeated, and why? • What historical stories would illustrate your point? • How can you defend the claim? How would you refute the claim?

The Six Facets of Understanding *(cont.)*

Facets of Understanding	Tasks and Questions for Students
Facet 3: The student has the ability to apply The student solves new problems or accurately applies the information in novel circumstances.	• How could you use what you have learned in new circumstances and diverse contexts? What are some possible situations that could arise where this knowledge would be useful? • What other types of problems could you solve with this knowledge? • How does this problem connect to another problem? How could you approach this new problem? How would you solve this problem? How would you explain this problem?
Facet 4: The student has gained new perspectives The student shows objectivity by logically examining and critiquing ideas from different vantage points.	• Explain and critique different points of view on the subject. • Reveal questionable assumptions and draw conclusions about what you have learned. • How would you describe some different points of view? • How does point of view impact the interpretation of the data? • What assumptions are being made? • How would you debate a different point of view? • Is there ever an absolute "truth"? Why or why not? • Why is this idea controversial? • Is there such a thing as totally accurate or objective reporting? Why or why not?

The Six Facets of Understanding *(cont.)*

Facets of Understanding	Tasks and Questions for Students
Facet 5: The student has the ability to empathize The student finds, explains, and respects the value in what others may find strange, unlikely, upsetting, or illogical.	• Imagine another person's perspective, or a different world view. How would that person feel? How would you justify that person's perspective? • Pretend that you are a different race/ethnicity/ socioeconomic status. How would you feel about this issue, and why? • What counter arguments might be used against you?
Facet 6: The student has self-knowledge The student reflects on his or her learning style, revealing personal blind spots, or explaining uncertainties that impact understanding.	• Be metacognitive and reflect on your own thinking. What was motivating you? • How did your personal viewpoint ultimately shape your understanding? • What conditions will help you learn? • Do you prefer to hear or to read information? • Would you rather write about something, act it out, do a puzzle, perform an experiment, or solve a problem? • How can you help yourself if something is hard to understand? • Are your feelings about…affecting your learning? • What prejudices do you have about…? Do your feelings shape your understanding? • What pro and con arguments would you make, and why?

Now that we have considered different ways that our students can demonstrate their understanding, two important questions remain: How can we structure our teaching to enable students to reach this understanding? How can we help students construct meaning from the work they do? In order to examine these questions thoughtfully, it is helpful to look at them from a historical perspective.

How We Construct Meaning: Constructivist or Project-Based Learning

For over 100 years, psychologists such as Jean Piaget, educators such as John Dewey, and educational theorists such as Lev Vygotsky have reported the benefits of experiential, hands-on, student-directed learning. The idea is that to gain understanding, students must construct meaning from their work rather than passively sit back and receive information from others. Merely parroting back information does not create deep understanding.

Understanding increases when students actively use what they know to explore, negotiate, interpret, create ideas, or investigate solutions to problems. True learning occurs when the learner solves problems and constructs solutions. In order for teachers to increase student understanding, they must shift the emphasis from having students memorize answers, to having them actively involved in thinking through problems and coming up with ideas and solutions themselves. Teachers need to give students the time and resources they need to think and explore. For example, students could design and perform an experiment to show whether heavy objects fall faster than light ones, determine under what conditions an object's weight might make a difference in the speed in which it falls, and figure out why—rather than just memorize the known answers to those questions.

The roots of project-based learning (PBL) lie in this constructivist tradition (Harris and Katz 2000). The term *project* does not necessarily mean that students create a physical structure; it means that students grapple with real questions and problems in order to construct meaning in their own minds. Although rooted in the theories of Piaget, Dewey, and Vygotsky, the true emergence of constructivist learning is the result of workplace readiness studies that were conducted over the last 30 years.

In the 1970s and 1980s, students who were entering the workplace relatively unprepared for work were a growing cause of concern. Traditionally, there had been a great disconnect between what students were taught in schools and what was necessary to successfully participate in the work force as adults. In 1990, Elizabeth Dole (who was then the U.S. Secretary of Labor) formed the Secretary's Commission on Achieving Necessary Skills (SCANS).

The purpose of this commission was to examine the demands of the workplace, and to determine how to structure learning so that young people would be ready to meet these demands. The commission was asked to do several things. They had to define the skills and the habits of mind (or personal qualities) needed for employment. This included what was necessary for students to be prepared for the workplace, what knowledge and skills they needed to possess, and what traits they needed to have to work effectively with others. The commission was also asked to propose acceptable levels of proficiency, suggest effective ways in which teachers could assess it, and develop strategies for teaching these proficiencies in schools.

The SCANS researchers conducted lengthy interviews with employers and workers. They analyzed the information received from a wide range of public and private employers, union leaders, business owners, supervisors, as well as workers in businesses, plants, and stores. They found that successful workers needed to have solid foundations in literacy, mathematics, and thinking skills. Workers also needed to have certain personal qualities such as dedication, cordiality, cooperation, responsibility, responsiveness, flexibility, and trustworthiness. They needed to be able to manage resources, work with others productively, acquire and use information, master complex systems, and work with new technologies.

This report on workplace readiness skills became a blueprint for education groups at all levels. If any nation was to be successful in the global economy, their students needed to learn the skills and competencies necessary for success in the workplace. Worldwide research in neuroscience and psychology bolstered the importance of these findings. The research showed that learners needed to construct meaning in order to understand new concepts, and that learning is at least partially a social activity; it takes place within the context of culture, community, and experiences.

The researchers recommended that one way to learn the skills needed to meet the demands of the workplace is to have students work together on group projects. However, they found that not all projects were equal. Simply making things was not enough. They determined that completing disconnected activities, making objects following specific directions, or solving predetermined problems did not necessarily help students gain a greater understanding of what they were learning or give them the ability to apply what they learned in new situations. Students had to work on projects where they could actively make meaning from the work that they performed.

True constructivist learning happens through projects that are problem-focused and central to the curriculum. Students come to conclusions based on their own investigations. In order to understand what a constructivist project is, it is helpful to see what it is not. A constructivist project does not have a predetermined outcome. In true project-based learning, projects are not scripted or packaged. Therefore, lab exercises where students follow scripted step-by-step procedures are not examples of PBL. Projects must be genuinely challenging: "If the central activities represent no difficulty and can be carried out with already known information and skills, the project is not PBL" (Thomas 2000).

Students can only create meaning from work that they do themselves. Too often, adults do the work for the children. Projects that only parents or teachers can do are not PBL. I remember a student I had years ago who handed in an exceptionally beautiful project. When I complimented her on it, she said, "Thank you. My mother wouldn't let me touch it!" As Harry Wong (1998; 2001) famously quipped, the person who does the work is the one who does the learning, but just think of who comes out exhausted from school at the end of the day. Usually, it's the teacher, not the students!

Project-based learning is a new way to think about projects. Traditionally, teachers had always assigned projects to students to extend or enhance the curriculum. They may have been assigned to provide illustrations, examples, additional practice, practical application, or enrich what was being taught. For example, a second grader might have read a book about a dinosaur, stuck a plastic dinosaur into a shoebox, glued in green and brown paper cut-outs as trees and grass, and called it a project.

However, that is not the type of project that enhances deep understanding. Rarely did students explore meaningful ideas through traditional projects. Seldom were these projects authentic or at the heart of the curriculum. Human brains need active engagement to learn. Students can't just sit passively and receive information that will magically lead them to the enduring understanding of complex ideas. They need to be actively involved in the learning process. They need to investigate real issues and problems.

True project-based learning requires a paradigm shift. A teacher's main role changes from being responsible for imparting information, to facilitating student-centered learning. The students make meaning by investigating open-ended, essential (or guiding) questions. This is not to suggest the elimination of direct teaching. Sometimes, direct lessons are the most efficient way to provide students with the information and skills necessary to investigate new ideas and information accurately and effectively. According to Jamie McKenzie (1998), "A good teacher knows when to act as 'sage on the stage' and when to act as a 'guide on the side.'" Because student-centered learning can be time consuming and messy, efficiency will sometimes argue for the sage. The role of the teacher shifts when students are busy making up their own minds. When exploring, problem solving, and investigation become the priority classroom activities, the teacher becomes a "guide on the side."

In student centered, project-based learning, teachers act primarily as facilitators through most of the process. They provide the structure for student exploration. Students have more choice, autonomy, and responsibility than in traditional instruction or traditional project work. Teachers must set clear expectations and make sure that the learning that takes place is well-organized and productive. McKenzie (1998) provides a list of descriptors of the role of a teacher who is acting as guide on the side: "The teacher is circulating, redirecting, disciplining, questioning, assessing, guiding, directing, fascinating, validating, facilitating, moving, monitoring, challenging, motivating, watching, moderating, diagnosing, trouble-shooting, observing, encouraging, suggesting, watching, modeling, and clarifying." Thus, the teacher is continually on the move. The teacher must assess student understanding on an ongoing basis so that he or she can provide continual customized and individualized support, feedback, and coaching. The teacher must continually check over students' shoulders, ask questions, and teach mini-lessons to individuals and groups who need specific skills. The teacher must set clear guidelines and benchmarks that will enable students to grapple with issues around the big ideas of the topic(s) which they are studying.

How the teacher sets up this structure is of paramount importance. Student investigations must be meaningful, motivating, and doable. According to Donna Walker Tileston's, *What Every Teacher Should Know About Learning, Memory, and the Brain* (2003), all learning seems to start with what she calls the "self-system of the brain" or the "system that decides whether or not to engage in learning." This requires the brain to make several determinations about incoming information. And Marzano, Pickering, and Pollock (2001) add, "If the task is judged important (satisfies a personal need or goal), if the probability of success is high (the student feels that past experience proves he/she can be successful) and a positive affect is generated or associated with the task, the individual will be motivated to engage in the new task."

Conclusion

The culmination of a true constructivist learning experience can take many forms but the key is that it is authentic, and that students demonstrate real mastery of the central concepts of the subject or topic that they are learning. Remember, lessons must be crafted so that students come to a deep understanding of central concepts through active investigation. The very best projects are those that have actual value outside the classroom. Ultimately, students are most motivated when they can use what they have learned in ways that positively impact others, especially those in their local communities.

Reflection

1. How could the Backwards Planning model help you plan your instruction so that your students achieve the desired goals?

2. According to Jamie McKenzie (1998), "a good teacher knows when to act as 'sage on the stage' and when to act as 'a guide on the side.'" What are some topics that you teach that would lend themselves to problem-based learning (or constructivist) teaching? How could you structure teaching so that your students can construct meaning from what they do?

3. How can you use the six facets of understanding to ask meaningful questions of your students? How might you encourage your students to deepen the quality of their responses?

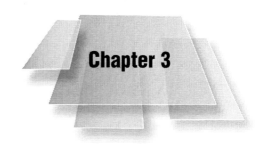

Chapter 3

What to Consider Before Planning a Unit of Study

We Learn

*10% of what we **READ***

*20% of what we **HEAR***

*30% of what we **SEE***

*50% of what we **SEE and HEAR***

*70% of what we **DISCUSS***

*80% of what we **EXPERIENCE***

*95% of what we **TEACH OTHERS***

—William Glasser

In determining which units of study to develop for deep understanding, some of the considerations to keep in mind are purely practical while others are theoretical. Ask yourself:

- Which topics that you teach merit in-depth student exploration?

- What material can be more effectively taught through direct instruction?

- What subject matter can be safely left out of the curriculum?

Before examining the factors that will help you determine what subjects and topics merit in-depth teaching, let's look at the idea of breadth versus depth of knowledge.

Breadth Versus Depth

A curriculum that emphasizes a huge breadth of material over depth of knowledge may actually stop students from gaining a deep understanding. What happens to students when the curriculum that is presented is "a mile wide and an inch deep"? There is not enough time to learn everything, and attempting to cover too much can be detrimental. Different industrial nations have different philosophies when it comes to breadth versus depth of knowledge. Some countries, such as the United States, promote a broad liberal education, while most countries in Europe and Asia have students specialize at a younger age. When schools feel compelled to include more information in all subject areas and require students to study each subject every year, the danger of covering too much material is that students are just skimming the surface. Without time to think about, explore, and understand material in depth, rigor and understanding will be sacrificed.

The Quick-Fix Failure

We may compound the problem of emphasizing breadth over depth of knowledge by our reaction to it. When students do poorly on high-stakes assessments (because we have tried to cover too much too quickly, resulting in students understanding too little) the trend is to fix the problem by concentrating on specific test preparation skills. When this is the reaction, students may learn how to perform somewhat better on the specific assessment for which we are preparing them, but their improved performance has little real value. It certainly does not mean that they have increased their depth of understanding. We need to realize that this type of quick fix reaction just exacerbates the problem because we are taking valuable time from teaching students underlying principles and skills. It is as preposterous as preparing a loved one for a physical exam before going to the doctor so that any health issues he or she might have can be masked instead of addressed!

That said, there is a limited amount of time available during the school day in which we have multiple goals we need to accomplish. As educators, we need to set priorities and make decisions about what we teach, how much time we will devote to each topic, and the instructional techniques that each topic merits.

Topics and Subjects to Teach with Breadth

Not everything students learn requires in-depth teaching, and there are many things to consider when deciding which topics to teach in depth. Practical considerations could include everything from specific national, district, or school expectations to the time of the year when you are teaching a particular topic. They can range from the materials, technology, and resources you have available, to the special school events and interruptions that are an endemic part of school life. Considerations can include your comfort level and experience with this type of teaching, or with a particular subject or topic, or it may include the constraints of your school's schedule.

You must first determine your purpose for teaching different aspects of the curriculum. Then think about the type, complexity, and importance of the different topics involved. You need to organize the concepts that you teach in ways that help students make appropriate connections. For example, if you are teaching chemical reactions based on the properties of different elements, you should organize this work so that your students study elements with similar properties (and thus similar reactions) together. Not every topic you teach needs to be geared to teaching for deep understanding. Many essential skills are taught more efficiently through simple explanation and practice. It may be helpful to think in terms of which skills and competencies require automaticity, which are foundational or necessary for students to know how to do in order to acquire knowledge, and which are at the heart of the topics we want our students to understand.

Skills Requiring Automaticity

There are things that students must learn how to do quickly and automatically, and some of these concepts, ideas, and information are fundamentally rote. For example, all students need to learn basics like the alphabet, sound-letter correspondence, and the multiplication tables. Being able to recall these quickly, easily, and accurately frees their minds to be thoughtful about other things. For example, if students can automatically decode written text, they do not need to expend their energy on sounding out words, and can therefore grapple with the meaning of that text.

However, not everything we ask students to memorize is helpful to them. It is not useful to have students memorize things that they will not use repeatedly. For example, learning the names of all of the capitals of different regions, states, or countries, or the names of all the leaders of a particular country wastes valuable time; students do not need these facts often, can easily look them up, and are likely to forget them quickly. It is also not useful to have students perform lengthy procedures that can easily be done by machines; such as pages of long division computations. (My youngest son was very happy when I convinced his fourth grade teacher not to give the class endless numbers of these problems every night.) However, gaining automaticity is crucial if students need to use a particular skill often.

Tasks that require memorization and automaticity can effectively be addressed through teacher presentations, examples, discussion, analysis, and lots of student practice. Some rote skills, such as letter formation or keyboarding, require only demonstration and practice. The best way to teach skills such as punctuation, spelling, and grammar is to have students practice those skills in a manner that replicates their use in the real world. For example, it is more effective to teach students to spell correctly, increase their vocabulary, and write grammatically by examining and analyzing what they read and write than it is to have them waste time by filling out spelling, vocabulary, and grammar worksheets that teach discrete skills out of context. It should not surprise you to hear that students who learn skills in such a disconnected manner can rarely transfer that knowledge to other contexts.

Foundational Skills

Foundational skills are the skills that students must have in order to acquire more information, solve problems, and communicate what they know. For example, students need to learn how to read with deep understanding. They need to know how to express their ideas clearly in writing, how to compute in order to solve problems, and how to present their ideas. Foundational skills require strategy teaching and lots of student practice.

Topics and Subjects to Teach with Depth

Topics that merit in-depth study are ones that are critical for understanding the subjects we are teaching, and thus, are worthy of thorough investigation. These topics are not necessarily easy to grasp, but they have relevance in the real world. They contain the big ideas that are basic to a subject. Therefore, if we structure our unit of study around them, students will be able to organize new information around these ideas. The connections students make will give them a greater understanding of how the world works and will help them to solve real problems.

Wiggins and McTighe (1998) present a set of questions to help teachers determine the broad goals or big ideas of instruction.

Three of these questions are particularly valuable:

- How critical is this information?

- How can we best make use of the discipline being studied?

- To what extent does this learning have value beyond the classroom?

The best essential questions are those that honestly need answers:

- Can one person effect meaningful change?

- How does music elicit emotion?

- How does corruption increase the cost of governmental systems?

- How does a person's point of view affect how he or she deals with change or conflict?

- How are scientific theories confirmed by experimental evidence?

- How can I use what I know about number relationships to develop efficient strategies to answer problems?

These questions will engage students in active, critical inquiry and help them see the significance of the topics that they are studying.

On All Levels: Teach for Transfer of Knowledge

Students, like adults, need to see the point of what they are doing. They need to know how they can use what they are learning outside of the classroom. The best way to do this is to demonstrate when, where, how, and why they will use what they learn, and then, provide opportunities to apply their knowledge to real-life problems. Knowledge that you can transfer or use in different conditions is called *conditionalized knowledge*. Unfortunately, this does not come naturally. Students often feel a disconnect between computations they perform in school and the real mathematics they encounter in everyday life. Students may use calculators to get answers, but they need to understand the underlying reasons for using particular algorithms when faced with a new problem.

Having students solve real world problems or compute authentic answers will have a more powerful impact than simply doing pages of computations. Suppose students are asked to design a play area for their schoolyard. They could start by measuring the yard. They could conduct a survey asking students what they wish to do during outdoor recess, and graph the results. They could then calculate the cost of equipment, design a scaled map for the area, figure out ways that the student body could raise money to buy the equipment, and present their findings to the principal and school board. This would be highly motivational and require both mathematical thought and computational skills.

In Planning for Enduring Understanding, Less Is More

When deciding which topic(s) to develop, remember that in terms of learning, less is often more (especially when it is covered in more depth). You will need to prioritize, but you may not have a choice about some of the breadth of information you are required to teach. Allan Collins (1996) proposed a workable solution to this dilemma: "A possible compromise between breadth and depth is to pursue a few topics in depth, while broadly covering a wide variety of topics." But "covering" does not mean simply hearing or memorizing disconnected facts. Thinking and solving problems depends on a deep, connected body of factual knowledge that is organized around important concepts.

You Design the Curriculum

You are the professional, and you have important decisions to make. You design the curriculum that you teach. You will need to make important decisions about what you teach, how you teach it, and why you teach it that way. If you pursue a few important topics in depth, and carefully plan your units of study with a clear purpose in mind, your students will have the time to organize their thoughts and make the necessary connections to truly understand those topics. Keep in mind that the key to teaching for enduring understanding is to make sure that your students can construct meaning and glean big ideas from their daily work.

Think About It

Much of what is taught in school leads to *inert knowledge*. Students can use what they learn to solve only the specific problems that they are given in school, but cannot transfer their knowledge to new contexts. Students' natural ability to transfer what they learn is over estimated by many teachers. It is our hope that students will be able to use what we teach them automatically and accurately; however, there has been fascinating research about this that has proven otherwise.

Perfetto, Bransford, and Franks conducted one particularly interesting study in 1983. They gave college students a number of "insight" problems (or riddles) to solve. The subjects were divided into three groups. One group was given the riddles with no clues. The other two groups were given clues to read just a few minutes before they were given the riddles to solve. Of the two groups given the clues, one was explicitly told to use them. The other group was not given this instruction. Here are two of the riddles:

- Uriah Fuller, the famous Israeli superpsychic, can tell you the score of any baseball game *before* the game starts. What is his secret?

- A man living in a small town in the U.S. married twenty different women in the same town. All are still living, and he has never divorced one of them. Yet, he has broken no law. Can you explain?

What follows are the clues that applied to the above riddles. (As you can see, they are not just directly relevant to the riddles, they are the actual answers!)

- Before it starts, the score of any game is 0 to 0.

- A minister marries several people each week.

This study had surprising results. Only the group who was given clues *and* told to use them did well on the riddles. Students who were given clues but were not instructed to use them did just as poorly on the riddles as the group that did not receive any clues at all. This type of experiment has been replicated many times, and the common finding is that subjects do not typically transfer relevant information to new problems without explicit instruction on how, when, where, and under what conditions to do so.

This has important implications for effectively helping students transfer knowledge. The conditionalized knowledge is something that is natural, but might not happen until quite a long way down the road. Thus, if we want students to quickly and easily *transfer* information to new contexts, we need to directly show and explain to them where, when, and how they can use this new knowledge, give them lots of practice applying what they learn, and provide opportunities to reflect on the connections which they are making.

An Array of Implementation Schemes

The most important decision you will make when determining which topic or topics to develop for enduring understanding stems from knowing yourself and what you can comfortably accomplish. What is the best first step for you? If this is the first time you are designing a unit of study for enduring understanding, you should think about starting small.

It is also helpful to work with interested colleagues, if at all possible. It is feasible to work alone, but it's far better for teachers to work together so that they can bounce ideas off each other during both the planning and implementation stages. Much has been written about the idea of improving schools by creating professional learning communities in which teachers work collaboratively. According to Richard Dufour (2004), the main idea behind effective professional learning communities is the belief that all students can and must learn. When teachers pledge that the core mission of their school is to ensure student learning, profound changes can take place.

To create a professional learning community, the focus must shift from examining what the teachers are delivering to what the students are actually learning. Are the students actively engaged? Are they asking appropriate questions? Can they pinpoint where they get confused? Do they know how to seek help? Can they use their new knowledge appropriately? In other words, the professional community must examine the results of instruction. When schools have a culture of collaboration where teachers systematically reflect upon, discuss, and analyze what students are learning in order to improve instructional practices, positive change is possible.

Patrick Baccellieri's book, *Professional Learning Communities: Using Data in Decision Making to Improve Student Learning* (2010), outlines the transformation of a high-needs, low-performing elementary school in Chicago. The experience of this school could be used as a model for creating effective professional learning communities in other schools. At South Loop School, where Baccellieri was principal for five years, teacher learning stemmed from professional collaboration that was results driven. Teachers examined student data and used that data to improve instruction. Since the collaboration at South Loop was focused on what mattered most (student learning as the result of instruction), it was highly effective, and student achievement increased.

Obviously, if you are planning an in-depth unit of study with one or more colleagues, you will need to set aside the time to work together, brainstorm ideas, review resources and materials, and give and receive feedback. However, the extra time it takes to collaborate is well worth it. When two or more teachers are open to sharing ideas and hashing out differences, they can help each other build more effective practices.

It is helpful to dialogue with your colleagues about the ongoing successes and challenges of a unit as you teach. You can examine student work together, reflect on what is happening in the classroom, and support each other's efforts. As you seek feedback from your peers and use that feedback to modify your teaching, you will be able to make your practice more effective, and you will have a greater impact on your students. However, it is important to note that even if you work alone, there are ways of getting ongoing assistance. There are many books and resources (such as this one) that are available to help you formulate your ideas, and there are online groups that you can join for support.

Remember, if you are working with different grade levels, there needs to be horizontal and vertical curriculum alignment. Horizontal alignment refers to the consistency of meeting the content standards for a subject area within a particular grade level. Thus, if one of the standards in third grade is learning procedural writing, all of the classes in third grade might create a unit where the students design their own comical how-to books.

Vertical alignment refers to having a logical and consistent order for teaching the content in a subject area from one grade level to the next. This allows students to get the foundational skills they need before moving on to more complex content. So, if a school decided to help students hone their math skills by designing a multi-grade level Math Olympiad, the games, contests, problems, and puzzles would be based on the skills and grade level standards of all students involved.

Whether you work with colleagues or work alone to design a unit of study for enduring understanding, there are several questions that must be answered:

- What are your teaching goals? What is it that you want each student to learn?

- How will you know when each student has achieved the goals of instruction?

- What will you do when a student experiences difficulty learning?

You may also design a unit with a colleague that involves more than one subject, and you would then need to take the goals of all subjects involved into consideration. For example, if two middle school teachers designed a joint social studies and English project, they would need to make sure that the unit they created addressed the standards of both subjects.

On the following charts we show classroom ideas for creating Stage One of the Backwards Planning unit at different grade levels. (A template for designing your own units that includes all three stages is provided in Appendix C, page 163.)

Stage One: Single Discipline; Single Unit of Study; Conducted in One Classroom

Topic: _____ Play _____   **Grade Level:** _____ Kindergarten _____

Length of Unit of Study: _____ Three weeks _____

Content Standard(s): Understands that interactions among learning, inheritance, and physical development affect human behavior

Big Idea(s) or Enduring Understanding(s):	**Essential or Guiding Question(s):**
Playing is the work of childhood	What about playing has changed over time? What has remained the same, and why?
Specific Understandings: • What is play? • Humans are not the only animals that engage in play • Play helps us learn and practice skills	**Possible Misunderstandings:** • Play requires specific equipment • Children learn only through play

Learning Targets:

- Children analyze exactly what they learn through the use of different toys and games.
- Children interview parents and grandparents about the toys and games with which they played as children, and find out which skills these adults learned from their play.
- Children form an opinion about the value of play.

Culminating Activity:

Create a "Toy and Game Hall of Fame." Students select the toys and games that they feel will always be valuable (or will stand the test of time).

(Adapted from Genesee Community Charter School Curriculum, http://www.gccschool.org/about)

Stage One: Single Discipline; Single Unit of Study;
Conducted Across a Single Grade Level

Topic: _____Fairy tales_____ **Grade Level:** _____Second grade_____

Length of Unit of Study: _____Three weeks_____

Content Standard(s): Understands the main ideas and basic literary elements in fairy tales	
Big Idea(s) or Enduring Understanding(s): Understands ways authors construct stories so they can write their own original stories	**Essential or Guiding Question(s):** What makes a story a fairy tale?
Specific Understandings: The story elements of a fairy tale • characters • setting • plot points • moral or lesson	**Possible Misunderstandings:** • Fairy tales always have happy endings

Learning Targets:
- Children listen to and read different types of stories to determine story elements in general, and the distinguishing characteristics of fairy tales in particular.
- Children write and illustrate their own fairy tales.

Culminating Activity:
Students participate in a Fairy Tale Forest where they share their stories with others. They decorate a large area with original pictures from their fairy tale settings. Each student dresses up as a character from his or her story at a Fairy Tale Tree and reads aloud to visitors. At the culmination of the event, students describe the elements of fairy tales and explain how their stories were constructed.

Stage One: Single Discipline; Single Unit of Study; Conducted Across Grade Levels

Topic: _____Inventions_____ **Grade Level:** _____Middle school_____

Length of Unit of Study: _____One month_____

Content Standard(s): Knows that invention is the process of creating a new system or object out of an idea, while innovation is the process of modifying an existing system or object to improve it	
Big Idea(s) or Enduring Understanding(s): Necessity is the mother of invention	**Essential or Guiding Question(s):** How can a simple invention or innovation change the way that we live?
Specific Understandings: • What are the main reasons for innovation and/or invention? • What are some of the ways inventions have changed the quality of life for people throughout history?	**Possible Misunderstandings:** • Technology improves everything

Learning Targets:

• All students work individually or in groups to find a common problem that does not yet have a solution.

• Students design and build a simple invention or innovation to solve the problem.

• Students examine simple inventions (like the paper clip or sticky notes) and innovations (like slotted spoons, scoops, and ladles) to see how these devices solve specific problems.

• Students brainstorm new ideas such as edible dishes, or toothbrushes with bristles that brush front and back at the same time.

Culminating Activity:

Organize an Invention Convention where students do research to find a problem that they can solve with a simple invention or innovation. They may interview others about the problems they have and keep logs of problems they encounter, hear, or read about. At the Invention Convention, students present their inventions or innovations to local scientists and business leaders. They discuss how simple innovations and inventions can change their lives.

Stage One: Multidiscipline; School-wide Unit or Units of Study for Each Student, All Teachers, Across Content Areas

Topic: Societies and culture   **Grade Level:** High school

Length of Unit of Study: One semester

Content Standard(s): Understands that group and cultural influences contribute to human development, identity, and behavior

Big Idea(s) or Enduring Understanding(s):	**Essential or Guiding Question(s):**
The health of a society depends on meeting the long term needs of its people.	What makes societies survive and thrive? What problems can arise that may lead to the downfall of that society? What must societies do to promote a healthy culture in the future?
Specific Understandings: • What components of a culture contribute to human identity? • What external factors contribute to a cultural identity?	**Possible Misunderstandings:** • Wealthier and more technologically advanced societies have the best chance of survival.

Learning Targets:

• Students study a culture that had flourished at one time, but eventually collapsed, through the lens of the essential or guiding questions. Students study their chosen culture's history and government, agriculture, use/misuse of natural resources, cultural values, scientific advances, use of human potential, etc.

• Students determine which factors lead first to that culture's success and then to its ultimate failure in order to come up with some underlying principles that answer the essential questions. They then design a presentation to substantiate their claims.

Culminating Activity:

Design a Culture Exposition. Groups of students present their analyses to local government officials and delineate general principles about what it takes to promote a healthy culture.

Designing Your Own Units of Study

Over the course of the next several chapters, we take a close look at how to create meaningful units of study using Backwards Planning principles. The focus is on providing a detailed account of each design stage with specific examples and strategies to make the planning process as easy and efficient as possible.

Caution: The Process Is Recursive

Although the different stages of Backwards Planning have dedicated chapters in this book, the planning process is not always going to be linear. When you are doing the actual planning, working on one stage will often trigger ideas for the other stages. Just like home improvement, changing or fixing one thing almost always makes you want to change or fix something else.

Thinking Can Be Messy, but Don't Worry

Here is an example of how it might work: Say you are designing a unit of study on the qualities that distinguish some books as classics while other books are merely fads. At first, you are not completely clear about how you want to design the unit. You know that you want your students to be able to figure out (and defend) the elements that they think make some books classic. These might include the qualities that you think make books classics. You think that classic books touch upon the human experience, contain universal characters, are written with words that make the ideas dance before the readers' eyes, were the first of their kind, were influential to their era, or contain messages that speak to the human spirit. But you also want your students to come up with their own definitions.

You know that you want to create a community of readers in your classroom. You want your students to read several of the same classics so that they can refer to some common experiences, but you also want them to compare and contrast these books to others of their own choosing to determine specific classic qualities. At first you go back and forth, thinking of the essential questions that you want your students to answer, and these questions make you think of some of the common books that you want them to read. You then begin to think about the type of writing that you want them to produce, and what kind of evidence could substantiate their claims. That makes you think about how you could best assess what they know and are able to do. In this way, you naturally go back and forth between your design elements as you are planning.

Be Patient with Yourself

To teach effectively, you must always have your long-term goals firmly in mind. You must structure your units of study around how your students can best attain these goals. You will need to review your plans many times as you clarify your ideas. But even with the best plans, you will need to remain flexible as you teach. You should expect to make changes in your daily lessons as you continually assess the progress of your students, so that your instruction stays on target. It is important to remain reflective about your unit of study so that the final design is coherent and logical. In the end, the elements of all your units should be aligned so that your students gain a deep understanding of the big ideas of the topic or subject that you are teaching. It is unrealistic to expect to have a perfect plan the first time you design a unit of study using Backwards Planning. Remember, it is a complex, but worthwhile endeavor.

Conclusion

Backwards Planning is worth the time and effort it takes. In the long run, your hard work will pay off. You will make a difference in the lives of the students you teach, because your purposeful teaching will lead them to the enduring understandings you want them to have. What you do will have real quality. William Glasser defines quality in his article, "Quality, Trust, and Redefining Education" (1992):

"Quality is difficult to define precisely. It almost always includes caring for each other, is always useful, has always involved hard work on someone's part, and when we are involved with it as either a provider or a receiver, it always feels good. Because it feels so good, I believe that all of us carry in our heads a clear idea of what quality is for us."

We all went into teaching to help students. If we can structure our teaching for enduring understanding so that our students will be able to use what we teach throughout their lives, our teaching will have real quality and lasting value. It will move into a realm of what Tom Peters (1994) refers to as "uncompromising excellence."

Reflection

1. How does the teaching of facts or skills differ from teaching for enduring understanding? What are some of the ways, besides traditional assessments, in which your students can demonstrate true understanding of the subjects or topics you teach?

2. Think about your teaching style. Where are you already implementing constructivist principles in your teaching? What are other topics that you teach that merit student-centered, in-depth teaching?

3. A teacher's greatest resource can be his or her colleagues. What can you and your colleagues do to help create a culture of professional collaboration within your school?

4. What can you do to make sure that your teaching has lasting value?

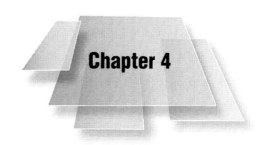

Chapter 4

Planning Units of Study with Your End Goal in Mind

The teacher keeps droning on about past participles and some kind of modifier. She goes on and on, and Jason catches a word here and there, but he cannot keep focused at all. School just seems pointless. Jason wants to graduate, and knows that his parents will be upset if he drops out, but what good is staying in school? If he drops out, at least he can make money and buy the stuff that he wants. Jason spends most of his time thinking about how to stay beneath the radar. Maybe if he's quiet, he won't get into trouble. Maybe if he looks down he won't catch the teacher's eye, and hopefully she won't call on him and embarrass him. Jason's overdue assignments are piling up, and he can't get himself to even look at them. Nothing that happens in class seems even remotely connected to his real life or what he is interested in. It's all boring, stupid, and pointless. Jason starts counting the days until his sixteenth birthday.

The mission of schools and educators should be to do more than merely cover content. It should be to do more than fill the days with endless disconnected activities, or spend countless hours drilling students in test preparation skills so that they can pass specific assessments. And certainly it should not be the goal of educators to simply make students better at going to school. The mission of schools should be to prepare students for the world beyond school. Students must understand that learning is a lifelong process, and that learning how to learn is the most important result of education.

Identify the Desired Results

Teachers need to help students gain knowledge, explore ideas, construct meaning, and reflect on their own thought processes and progress. Students need to be able to use what they learn in school to solve real-world problems, both now, and in the future. To help students do this, the design of instructional units must be results oriented.

Therefore, the first stage in the Backwards Planning process is to identify the desired results (or the goals) of your unit of study. This is the big picture stage where you need to think about exactly what enduring understandings, knowledge, and skills you want your students to acquire from what they are learning. In this chapter, we will examine ways to set goals for a unit of study.

Be Straightforward

In determining the desired results, it is best to be as straightforward and to the point as possible. It is not helpful to include a long laundry list of vaguely related goals, understandings, questions, and learning targets that you may or may not have time to address. In the end you only want to include the big ideas and essential questions that you want your students to explore in depth. And don't get discouraged. The extra time it will take you to plan this way at the beginning will make your teaching more powerful. It will also save you time in the long run because your day-to-day planning will be driven by your clear purpose.

Design Tools

In order to help you plan the desired results stage, and each of the others, Wiggins and McTighe provided "design tools" in their books to guide thinking. We will look at each of these goal-setting design tools individually. Some of these tools will be presented differently from the way Wiggins and McTighe presented them; however, the basic stages of planning remain the same. Each one is examined in depth over the next few chapters. When you are actually planning, you will naturally go back and forth between the different stages. And you do not need to feel compelled to use every design tool in a given stage. Just use the ones that suit your needs. The important thing is that you always keep the end result that you are seeking clearly in mind as you plan, so that you can align all of the parts of your unit of study.

A mnemonic that you may wish to use for creating powerful goals is SMART. SMART stands for goals that are Specific, Measurable, Attainable, Realistic, and Time-bound. William Levack, a New Zealand doctoral student, researched the origins of SMART goals in 2007–2008, and discovered that there is some controversy about who originated these concepts. There are even some differences in what the letters stand for. However, this mnemonic has become the cornerstone of goal setting in fields as diverse as business management and physiotherapy. It also has strong implications for education. Consider what you want your students to know and be able to do because of what they are learning. Once you have addressed this, you can plan with your final goal in mind. The chart on the following page examines each of the SMART attributes individually as they pertain to education.

SMART Goals

Specific

Since it is easier to attain a specific goal than a general one, your goal should be as clear and explicit as possible. To do this, you will need to decide what you want your students to accomplish, and why you want them to accomplish it. What are the specific reasons or purposes of a specific goal? What benefits will your students gain by reaching that goal? You also need to think about the requirements and constraints you are likely to face when teaching for a particular goal, and the specific time frame your students will need to reach it.

Measurable

You must determine what evidence you will need to prove that your students have met the final goal. There are several questions you can ponder: What criteria will you use to determine long-term success? How will you measure student progress along the way? How can you pinpoint the problems your students are experiencing so that you can help them?

Attainable

Attaining the goal is what will define success. You need to think about how you can help your students accomplish it. What skills, abilities, understandings, and attitudes will your students need in order to reach it? This will require you to carefully plan the steps that will enable your students to be successful. What strategies will you use to help students who are struggling or who are exceeding expectations?

Realistic

Your goals should represent substantial progress, but they must be realistic and doable. Interestingly, a lofty goal is often easier to attain than a mundane one, because often a lofty goal is intrinsically more motivating. However, you need to clearly understand what background information and skills your students already have, what they lack, and what they need next. Far-reaching goals must have specific, delineated steps that are achievable. Students must feel successful as they progress in order to remain motivated.

Time-bound

In order to give the goal a clear priority and to create a sense of urgency, it should be grounded within a specific time frame. How much time do you have available for the unit of study? What is the time frame your students will need to reach the goals of instruction?

A Few Words about High-Stakes Testing and Standards

In school systems where success is measured by high-stakes testing, and the schools themselves are judged by how well their students achieve on these tests, there is a great danger of instruction becoming almost solely organized around test preparation activities. Even high-stakes assessments that try to ensure that students meet rigorous standards tend to be repetitive from year to year. One thing is certain: Students will definitely lose when the scope of their education is reduced to only those things that will most likely appear on a single, specific, and often repetitive test.

There is little doubt, however, that standards themselves are crucial. Educational standards define the knowledge and skills students should possess at critical points in time. If you do not have "clear and rigorous" standards, and you have not determined what your students should "know and be able to do" (U.S. Department of Education 2001–2009), there is no reasonable way to measure the quality or effectiveness of what you are teaching.

Thus, as you begin planning your unit of study, it is important to review the applicable content standards for the subject or topic which you are teaching on the national or state level. You will also need to examine local content standards for your district or school. Think about the stated goals, objectives, and learning outcomes. Then determine how your unit of study will most effectively address these standards. This is not about test preparation. This is about ensuring that what you teach your students will enable them to reach clearly defined and appropriately challenging goals.

A Sample Unit on Ecology

In order to make the planning process clear, we will demonstrate how to develop a constructivist, student-centered unit of study. This middle school unit is written using the Backwards Planning format and is designed to lead students to an enduring understanding of the underlying principles behind ecology. Each of the components of this unit is detailed separately, and each is explained under the umbrella of the specific design tool used to develop it. The idea is for you to see how these components fit together so that you can use it as a sample for producing your own units of study. We will also look at examples from other grade levels and other fields of study to clarify the process.

The standards for this unit of study on ecology are taken from the Mid-continent Research for Education and Learning (McREL). McREL is a nonprofit organization that, among other things, lists a compendium of standards taken from subject-area organizations and from different states. Two of the science organizations linked to McREL are the American Association for the Advancement of Science and the National Science Teachers Association. The following McREL standards relate to the ecology unit we are developing.

Sample Ecology Unit

Content Standard(s)
- Understands the characteristics of ecosystems on Earth's surface
- Understands the sources and properties of energy
- Understands how human actions modify the physical environment

What enduring understandings do we want our students to acquire because of this unit of study? What guiding principles at the heart of this subject do we want our students to understand? What deep connections do we want our students to make and be able to use? What permanent impact do we want this unit to have on our students?

To determine the enduring understandings you want your students to acquire, think about the compelling "big ideas" at the heart of what you are teaching. According to Grant Wiggins' e-journal *Big Ideas* on his website http://www.authenticeducation.org/ae_bigideas/index.lasso, "a big idea" is any concept, theory, principle, or theme that helps learners make sense of a subject. Wiggins gives examples of "follow the money" as being a "big idea" in politics, and the "American Dream" as being a "big idea" in literature.

Although big ideas are deliberately framed as generalizations, Wiggins cautions that they are not just vague statements that refer to a broad amount of content, such as "change" or "outer space." It is more useful to think of big ideas as "organizing strategies or principles that will help students make sense of the information they are learning" (Wiggins, n.d.) First think about big ideas or guiding principles at the center or core of your unit of study, and then think about the specific understandings that you want your students to acquire around these big ideas. The students will use these general principles as a frame around which they will examine factual information and build a conceptual understanding.

Sample Ecology Unit

Big Idea(s) or Enduring Understanding(s)

All people are responsible for keeping Earth clean and safe so that it can continue to sustain life.

Specific Understandings

All life forms need food and energy.

- Certain natural resources are necessary for Earth to produce food and energy that sustains life such as, fresh air, clean water, and uncontaminated soil.

- Animal and plant life on Earth depend upon each other.

- When individuals' actions are solely based on their self interest, they may eventually destroy a shared, limited resource, even when it's against everyone's long-term interest to do so. However, individuals or groups can make and enforce rules for sharing and preserving the common resources that they all need (Hardin 1968).

- People's present habits are destroying some of Earth's natural resources.

- People need to adjust their lifestyles so that they do not further endanger Earth's natural resources.

Possible Misunderstandings

According to Bransford, Brown, and Cocking (1999), students' misconceptions hamper their understanding: "Students come to the classroom with preconceptions about how the world works. If their initial understanding is not engaged, they may fail to grasp the new concepts and information that are taught, or may learn them for the purposes of a test but revert to their preconceptions outside the classroom." In other words, if the new learning conflicts with your students' preconceived ideas, they may not study the topic with an open mind.

In order to help students reach key understandings about a topic, you need to think about how to avoid possible misunderstandings. You may consider these two questions:

- What misconceptions may your students already have about this subject?

- What misunderstandings are most likely to crop up as you teach?

To find out what misconceptions your students may initially have, ask them to write down or discuss what they think about the subject *before* you begin teaching. That way, you can then flag any preconceived erroneous notions, prejudices, misinformation, or confusion. The more you know about students' misconceptions, the better able you will be to resolve them in your instruction. This will help you structure your teaching so that your students can freely explore new information. In thinking about what misunderstandings are likely to crop up as you teach this topic, you will need to use what Bransford, Brown, and Cocking refer to as your "pedagogical content knowledge" (1999). Although you probably won't be able to predict all of the difficulties that may arise, thinking about some of the most likely potential problems will help you construct a stronger unit of study. If you determine the background information that your students may be missing, or which areas of your subject may be tricky or difficult, you can structure your teaching to nip potential problems in the bud.

Sample Ecology Unit

Possible Misunderstandings

- Some students may feel that conservation efforts will hinder human progress, and this idea may stop them from studying the unit with an open mind. Therefore, during the unit, you might deal with how humans can make use of natural and useable forms of energy that conserve natural resources while allowing for continued human progress.

- Some students may not have enough of a background in physical and Earth sciences to understand ecological problems that will be addressed. Some students may not know how using nonrenewable energy sources affects the elements needed to sustain life. Therefore, during the unit, you may need to provide specific lessons in such background information.

The chart below and on the following pages presents some examples of enduring understandings, specific understandings, and possible misunderstandings that you may use to develop units of study in other subject areas. Think about how the big ideas in the first column can be used as organizing principles for students to explore.

Examples of Big Idea(s) or Enduring Understanding(s) by Subject

Big Idea(s) or Enduring Understanding(s)	Specific Understandings	Possible Misunderstandings
Literacy		
A good storyteller rarely tells the meaning of the story.	• A reader must infer the meaning in a good story. • The author's purpose may be interpreted differently by different readers.	• A good storyteller never gives a straightforward message.
Classic books deal with truisms about human nature.	• Books must reveal some truth about human nature or they cannot hold their appeal over time • Even books that are not about humans can reveal truisms about human nature.	• There is only one "truth" about human nature.

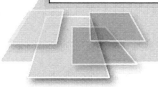

Examples of Big Idea(s) or Enduring Understanding(s) by Subject (cont.)

Big Idea(s) or Enduring Understanding(s)	Specific Understandings	Possible Misunderstandings
Social Sciences		
Friendships can be deepened or undone by hard times.	• Crises can bring out the best in people. • Crises can bring out the worst in people.	• Once a friendship is "undone," it can never recover.
In order for a justice system to be fair, it must be adversarial.	• In an adversarial justice system, both sides must be exaggerated to get to the truth. • "Truth" may depend on point of view.	• There can never be a clear right or wrong answer when it comes to justice.
Economics		
Price is a function of supply and demand.	• Competition lowers the cost of an item. • Value is dependent on the need for and the availability of a product or service.	• People can always buy things at their true value in a free market.
When people do not use natural resources wisely, they undermine the human condition.	• Earth only has a limited supply of the resources needed to sustain life. • Humans have a more detrimental effect on natural resources than any other animal.	• People can replenish all natural resources with artificial inventions.

Examples of Big Idea(s) or Enduring Understanding(s) by Subject *(cont.)*

Big Idea(s) or Enduring Understanding(s)	Specific Understandings	Possible Misunderstandings
Art and Music		
Great artists must break with conventions in order to make a lasting impression.	• We can learn about the values in a society by seeing how artists interpret the conventions of that society. • Great artists help people view the world in unusual ways.	• Great artwork can never be realistic.
One person's music is another person's noise.	• Greatness in music may be defined by cultural experiences. • Each generation has its own definition of great music.	• Music can be deemed "good" or "great" based solely on the elements it possesses.
History		
History is the story told by the "winners."	• Even textbooks may be written from a specific perspective. • Propaganda can sometimes be written as history.	• History books can tell the absolute truth.
Studying different time periods helps us to understand our own.	• Studying different time periods helps us to determine true human need. • There are things that are unique to different time periods, but human nature remains constant.	• We cannot change the course of history by examining the past, so why bother studying it?

Examples of Big Idea(s) or Enduring Understanding(s) by Subject *(cont.)*

Big Idea(s) or Enduring Understanding(s)	Specific Understandings	Possible Misunderstandings
Science		
Fossils give evidence of Earth's story.	• Geological changes in Earth caused the preservation of some plants and animals before they decomposed. • Remnants of plants and animals from previous times can be found in rocks.	• Fossils undermine all religious beliefs.
Multi drug-resistant bacteria and viruses are the result of human misuse of antibiotics and anti-viral drugs.	• Organisms adapt to the conditions in which they live in order to survive. • Survival of the fittest means that organism strains will develop adaptations that enable them to resist the antibiotics that we now use to kill them. This will make present antibiotics ineffective, and that is likely to cause great health problems in the future.	• Anytime you are sick you can take a pill to be cured.

Examples of Big Idea(s) or Enduring Understanding(s) by Subject *(cont.)*

Big Idea(s) or Enduring Understanding(s)	Specific Understandings	Possible Misunderstandings
Mathematics		
The better we understand mathematical principles, the more efficiently we can solve problems.	• Memorizing formulas does not necessarily help you to understand mathematical principles. • Understanding the underlying concepts in algebra or geometry helps you solve the problems you face in your daily lives. • When faced with novel problems, math experts first try to understand the nature of the problem and the underlying concepts behind it.	• Math is disconnected from real life. • Math is simply about solving problems as quickly and painlessly as possible. • Mathematical thinking is mainly about applying the right formula to each problem.
Health		
Good health depends on emotional as well as physical considerations.	• Peer pressure often adversely affects healthy choices. • Stress can cause health-related problems.	• Good health depends almost entirely on a person's genetic makeup.
Government		
A government's main goal is to stay in power.	• Power can be a corrupting force. • In a good government, officials do not promote stereotypes and prejudices.	• The only way to attain power is through corruption.

Choosing Essential or Guiding Questions

Students construct understanding as they grapple with the essential questions around the big ideas in the unit of study. In order for questions to be both essential and relevant, they need to foster the understanding that you want your students to seek. Following our ecology unit, we define one essential and several guiding questions.

Essential questions are open-ended and must be written in a way that students can understand. They resist a simple or single "right" answer, but instead provoke deep thought. They may be counterintuitive or controversial. They should involve students in substantive dialogue and debate. Essential questions can neither be answered quickly nor easily, but they are worth revisiting. In fact, they recur throughout life. They often raise important philosophical or conceptual issues, as they call upon students to consider both their content knowledge and their personal experiences. Essential questions should encourage creative and critical thinking, imagination, and curiosity. They should promote motivation for understanding. They should lead students to ask other questions, as they construct new meaning from what they are learning.

Thus, essential questions are concepts in the form of questions and should be written in broad terms. They serve as organizers and set the focus for a lesson or unit of study. Students must be able to understand them. Essential questions should be written in a logical sequence and should not be repetitious.

According to Heidi Hayes Jacobs, each essential question you choose should be "distinct and substantive" (1997). Jacobs thinks that essential questions reveal the intent of the teacher. When you choose an essential question, you are making a commitment. In effect you are saying, "This is our focus for learning. I will put my teaching skills into helping my students examine the key concept implicit in the essential question." Jacobs thinks that essential questions should act as organizers around which you structure "an array of activities" (1997). She cautions about the importance of developing essential questions that are "realistic," given the amount of time you have for your unit of study.

As students grapple with essential questions, they should be able to make insightful connections between seemingly disparate ideas, concepts, and facts. These guiding questions should cause students to think about how they might apply what they are learning in different contexts.

Sample Ecology Unit

Essential Question(s)

How can people keep Earth clean and safe so that it can continue to sustain life?

Guiding Questions (concepts necessary to explore main question)

- Why do we need an environmental balance to sustain life?

- How are the chemical elements that are essential to life continually recycled among and between organisms?

- How do human habits alter the ecosystem, and what are the possible short-term and long-term consequences of this?

- How can humans protect Earth's natural resources and still make progress?

- How can we prevent people and industries from poisoning our environment?

You may follow the steps in the planning guide on page 78 to help you in defining essential or guiding questions for your unit of study.

Essential or Guiding Question Planning Guide

Step	Reasoning
1. Write your main goal or objective as an essential question.	What enduring understanding(s) will students come to by exploring this essential question?
2. Determine what smaller key concepts your students will need to explore.	What connections will students need to make? How will students apply what they know and learn?
3. Write these key concepts into *guiding* questions that are understandable to students.	Turn each connection or application point into a separate question that needs to be answered.
4. Order the guiding questions logically or sequentially.	Consider ordering questions from most broad to most specific, or order questions so foundational knowledge is constructed first.
5. Discuss the guiding questions with your students to make sure that they understand them and make any necessary revisions.	Questions must be realistic and authentic in order to achieve buy-in from students.
6. Post the essential questions and the guiding questions in a prominent place.	Your students must get the continuous message that these questions are essential for them.

Some Other Sample Essential or Guiding Questions

The chart on page 79 delineates some sample essential questions in different content areas. As you read this chart, think about the concepts these questions represent. How might students explore these questions to understand the big ideas behind them? What smaller, related key questions should students explore to uncover the big concepts?

Sample Essential or Guiding Questions by Subject

Subject	Question
Literacy	• How does a good read differ from a great book? • What makes some books fads and others classics?
Social Sciences	• How can we as a society ensure that justice is served?
Economics	• How "rational" is the stock market and why?
Art and Music	• Should the arts ever be censored? Why or why not?
Geography	• How is a person's destiny determined by his or her geography?
History	• In what ways does history reflect the survival of the fittest?
Government	• What is the government's proper role in helping its people? • When is a government overstepping its bounds?
Science	• How does a plausible belief become a scientific theory?
Mathematics	• How can a person become more efficient in solving math problems?
Foreign Language and Culture	• How are a society's values and beliefs reflected in their native languages, religions, and cultures?
Health	• How do both genetics and environment impact health?
Physical Education	• How can appropriate exercises increase a person's health and well-being?

Establishing Learning Targets: What Students Will Know and Be Able to Do

Once you have determined the standards, big ideas, and the essential and guiding questions that will direct your unit of study, the next step is to determine your students' learning targets. According to Bransford, Brown and Cocking (1999), students must have a deep foundation of factual knowledge in order to develop competence in the area of inquiry. Furthermore, students must understand facts and concepts in the context of a conceptual framework. Knowledge that is organized in this way can be retrieved easily and used to solve problems. The question is, how do we help students achieve this? How do we determine the learning targets that we want our students to achieve?

Learning targets are what your students will know and be able to do by the end of the unit of study. Knowing and doing are related, but they are not the same things. Establishing specific learning targets will help guide you in developing lessons that will lead students to the goals of instruction. Keep the following questions in mind:

- What do your students already know, and what skills do they already possess that will help them answer the essential questions?

- What new skills and knowledge will your students need to answer the question(s)?

- What strategies can you use that will actively engage your students in exploring the concepts and working towards the answers?

- How will you know that your students understand the material? How will you pinpoint any confusion as students proceed?

- How will you support the students who are struggling? How will you enrich the experience for students who need extra challenges?

Remember that your final goal in teaching is to build understanding. But understanding cannot exist without accurate information. Students need a strong foundation of factual knowledge. Facts are the data needed for understanding. But if facts are taught in a didactic and disconnected way, they will not lead to understanding. So you must determine what information your students will need in order to form an understanding. Think about what your students must know that will help them form a conceptual framework around the big ideas of your unit of study. Consider these two questions:

- What enabling facts, concepts, and principles will help your students investigate answers to the essential questions of your unit?

- How can this knowledge best be organized to help students build a strong framework of understanding?

Sample Ecology Unit

Learning Targets—Enabling Knowledge (What Students Will Know)

- key factual information on what both animals and plants need to live

- factual information on how people's habits permanently alter the air, water, and land

- short-term and long-term consequences of using natural resources in ways that are unsustainable

- the renewable natural resources that can be used for energy

- how people can use renewable energy in practical ways

- what specific ecological problems exist in students' communities

- practical suggestions for solving some of the community's ecological problems

Next, you need to determine what your students will be able to do as a consequence of your unit of study. Students need to have skills—or in other words—particular procedures, strategies, and methods that will enable them to apply their knowledge. Students can demonstrate understanding when they are able to take what they know and apply it to do, make, explain, present, interpret, or solve something.

Sample Ecology Unit

Learning Targets—Enabling Skills (What Students Will Be Able to Do)

- show different ways in which plants and animals provide life-sustaining materials for each other

- perform an experiment that demonstrates the consequences of using resources in ways that are not sustainable

- construct a model or make a poster that demonstrates how a renewable energy resource works

- research some of the ecological problems in the community

- write an article about at least one of the ecological problems in the community and ways in which community members can work together to solve that problem

- present findings in a creative and memorable way

Developing the Culminating Activity

We do not gain enduring understanding by passively sitting back and listening to big or important ideas or merely memorizing facts. Human brains need engagement to learn. As we make connections, we construct a neural framework of understanding in our brains. This framework is permanent, while memorized facts will quickly be forgotten.

Students' motivation increases when they are involved in authentic investigations. By authentic, we mean that the work they do has value beyond the classroom. Students become highly motivated when they know that they are grappling with essential questions that honestly need answers. Our students will be inspired to work hard if they know that the work that they do can be of real benefit to those around them, especially if it helps people in their own communities.

Authentic problems are easy to find anywhere. (In fact, they often find you!) If at all possible, it would be best to select a project or culminating expedition that is related to a real problem that affects your school or local community.

If you want to structure your unit of study so that your students are highly motivated to demonstrate their mastery of the central concepts, you should design a culminating event in which students can showcase the results of their work. And, if that culminating event has value beyond the classroom, you will be achieving the gold ring of teaching!

Remember, The Process Is More Important than the Product

When you plan the culminating event, you will need to be cautious about one thing: It is the process of exploring and uncovering the big ideas that are at the heart of the unit of study that is key. The integrity of that *process* is what determines what the students will ultimately learn, remember, and be able to use. Although we want our students to showcase thoughtfully presented projects and presentations, the process of learning is always what is most important. The students must do the exploration, deep thinking, and hard work required to produce the presentations and projects themselves. One of your roles as a teacher will be that of a quality controller. But you cannot do the work for your students so that the culminating products look good. Remember, the ones who do the work do the learning, and that always must be the students!

Notice how a culminating project like this pulls the unit of study together. The students have the opportunity to explore the topic of ecology in depth, grapple with its essential questions, form a deep understanding about different aspects of the topic, and use what they have learned to do something that is authentic and that can positively impact their communities.

Sample Ecology Unit

Culminating Activity: Teach-in

The students will work in groups to teach the community members about the ecological issues that affect our lives, and what we can all do to protect the environment in which we live. Students may prepare displays with explanatory essays, skits, debates, slide shows, songs, dances, and/or other presentations. Their displays and presentations will include information on the survival needs of animals and plants, how plants and animals depend on each other to sustain life, and how some human habits (such as the use of nonrenewable energy sources) can change ecosystems permanently. The students will distribute an original magazine, *It's Not Too Late: How We Can Save Our Local Environment* in which they detail some local problems and present some specific ways that community members can help solve these problems. Students will ask community members to make a commitment to the environment in at least one way that they have not done previously. Student projects will be displayed at the local library, and a copy of the magazine will be donated to the library for its collection.

Here are some examples of possible culminating projects across the curriculum:

Subject	Culminating Activity
Civics	Students write a proposal and draw up plans to change a local vacant lot into an environmentally-sound public park that serves different age populations.
Mathematics	Students set up a school store and use the profits from it to buy books and toys for the pediatric wing of a nearby hospital.
English/ Language Arts	Students write poetry and make picture books for younger students in the school system.

Conclusion

The first stage in creating a unit of study based on Backwards Planning is the "big idea" stage. You need to think carefully about exactly what you want the results of your instruction to be. What enduring understandings do you want your students to acquire through your unit of study? What worthy, essential questions should your students investigate and explore? What previous misconceptions might hamper their understanding? What specific knowledge and skills will they need? How can you make their learning authentic and motivating? What culminating project will give them an opportunity to demonstrate that they have met the goals of instruction? Once you know where you want your students to end up, you can carefully map out your plans for helping them get there.

Reflection

1. What are some essential questions that will guide your students to the big ideas of a topic or subject that you are teaching?

2. According to Bransford, Brown, and Cocking (1999), "Students come to the classroom with incorrect preconceptions about how the world works. If their initial understanding is not engaged, they may fail to grasp the new concepts and information that they are taught, or may learn them for the purposes of a test but revert to their preconceptions outside the classroom." How can you determine some common misconceptions that your students may have about a topic that you teach? How can you address these possible misunderstandings in your instruction?

3. How can you structure a culminating project so that it is authentic and so that your students are accountable for demonstrating that they have attained the goals of instruction? Does your grading system accommodate this method of instruction?

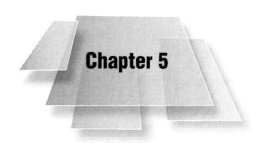

Chapter 5

How Assessments Can Help You Target Your Teaching

Imagine the following scenario:

It is near the end of the semester. Mr. Brown has to submit his final grades, and frankly, he's worried. He has several "stars" who answer questions correctly in class, do their homework regularly, and who like to participate. Many of his students just seem to sit there, and some of them are obviously disinterested. Three of them have their own agendas, and they are downright disruptive and rude. Mr. Brown has few formal grades for his students. He is in a quandary. He knows he doesn't have much time to mark their work now, so he decides to assign a short paper and to give a multiple-choice test. He's pretty confident about what the results will be. But with a few graded assignments, he feels he can avoid accusations of being unfair. The assessments don't take too much time to mark. However, he is horrified when he sees the poor quality of all of the students' short essays, and he is dismayed when he realizes that even some of his stars have bombed the test. Now it's too late to do anything about it.

learly Mr. Brown made an assumption that the students who actively participated in his class knew the material, and he would be able to reward them with good grades. Unfortunately, because he did not evaluate his students regularly, he had no idea about their proficiency or understanding. Therefore, he could not structure his teaching to actually help his students learn.

Making Informed Decisions

How do we know what students are ready to learn? How do we know how to teach them? The answers lie in continually assessing and addressing what students know, what they are confused about, and what they are able or unable to do. We cannot effectively instruct our students unless we take a careful account of their knowledge base and skill level on an ongoing basis. Every teacher struggles with how to assess students accurately, fairly, and efficiently. When the purpose of instruction is enduring understanding, ongoing assessment is vital to provide the information that both teachers and students need to make subsequent teaching, learning, and understanding possible.

It is common to see ongoing assessment in teaching situations outside the regular classroom. For example, when a conductor is practicing with an orchestra, he must be able to hear the orchestra as a whole, as well as the different instrumental sections and the individual players. He needs to see if the members of the orchestra are coming in at the exact right time, playing the notes correctly, paying attention to the musical cues, and staying in tune. If the piece has lyrics, the conductor would need to see that the way the music is played reflects the mood and interpretation of those lyrics. The conductor might pay special attention to a particular facet of the music that he wants the orchestra to improve, but he would need to remain continually alert to all aspects of playing. It is only through careful analysis of what the musicians are doing at all times that the conductor can tailor what he's doing to help the orchestra play the piece correctly.

But if the goal were true musicianship (i.e., an enduring understanding of how music should be played), adequate technical performance of the piece would not be enough. In order to help the orchestra achieve musicianship, both the conductor and musicians would need to be vigilant. The conductor would have to be cognizant of what each member could or could not do at any given time and give appropriate feedback. He might need to have sectional rehearsals and provide individual help. He would have to continually guide the musicians, give them feedback on their successive performances, backtrack when necessary, and proceed to more advanced concepts when they were ready. The musicians would need to practice and rehearse the techniques, internalize the feedback, and use it to increase their musicianship and performance level. (Maybe with the right teaching and enough practice, the orchestra might finish off their Carnegie Hall debut with a standing ovation!)

Students also need clear and continual feedback if they are to overcome any confusion that might prevent them from forming deep understandings. They need to know when they are on track and when they are veering off. Appropriate feedback can help students deepen their knowledge base and skill level, make appropriate connections, and apply their learning in novel situations. Feedback can help them transform the quality of their thought and of their work. The question is, how can this be done effectively and efficiently, given the numbers of students for which teachers are responsible? One thing is certain: To get an accurate and complete picture of what your students know and can do, you will need a multi-faceted approach to data collection.

Using Multiple Measures: The Snapshot Versus the Photo Album

If you ever look through old family photo albums, you might be surprised to see how much you've changed over various ages and stages in your life. All humans are dynamic; they continually change based on both internal and external factors. There is probably no one picture that can truly define who you are. However, if your albums were filled with many different types of pictures over time, their totality would obviously provide a more accurate account of who you are than just a single snapshot.

Getting a clear picture of a student's skill set in school requires different types of assessments. Not all assessments need to be formal, and not all of them need to be pencil and paper. Some just require thoughtful observation of a student's words or actions. However, a one-time snapshot is *never* enough. Students constantly grow and change. Teachers need ongoing information in order to tailor instruction in a meaningful way. Without taking continual stock of what students know and are able to do, your instruction will likely become hit or miss. Teachers need to provide students with a variety of ways to demonstrate their understandings, and they need to give students clear and specific feedback about what it would take to improve their next performance.

Thus, the teacher must determine the acceptable evidence that will prove that their students are achieving the desired results of the unit of study. In the words of Grant Wiggins and Jay McTighe (2005), this requires that the teacher "think like an assessor." The teacher must decide "what to look for to determine the extent of student understanding". Teachers must figure out the evidence that will give them the most specific information about how well their students are meeting the learning targets that they outlined in Stage One. Teachers must use a multitude of measures to get a clear and ongoing picture of student understanding. Teachers also need to determine how this data can help guide their instruction.

There are several key issues here. First, think about the goals of your unit of study. What are your students' learning targets? Then determine how to best assess each of those learning targets. Think about what student data you can glean through written assessments, performance-based assessments, and careful observations of what your students say and do. It is important to carefully match each assessment with your purpose for giving it. For example, if one of your learning targets is that students explain the processes they use to solve a math problem, they should be required to explain all of their work when you assess them.

Finally, determine how you will use the data you collect to adjust and target your instruction based on your students' needs. If the information you collect gives you a clear and specific picture of what your students know and can do and what confusions they have, it will help you differentiate instruction. The data will enable you to develop both effective intervention strategies for students who do not meet the objectives, as well as enrichment and acceleration strategies for those who exceed the objectives.

Types of Assessments

Formal and informal assessments may cover a wide gamut of skills. But before we go any further, it might be helpful to define the different types of assessments and what they reveal.

Screening assessments are usually administered to students early in the year, or they may be administered at the beginning of a unit of study. They are generally used to identify which children are on or above grade level, and which ones are weak in specific skills and knowledge, thereby requiring additional support to succeed. (Think in terms of a health screening to determine the possible diseases a person may have.) Examples of screening assessments are pretests before a unit of study or a pre-kindergarten or kindergarten readiness checklist.

Diagnostic assessments provide more detailed information about the nature of the deficits for students who are not progressing. They are administered to determine the reasons for a lack of progress, which are not always apparent. Diagnostic testing is only required when information from other assessments is insufficient to explain a student's learning difficulties. These tests are usually given by trained professionals.

Formative assessments are used to inform instruction. They may be formal or informal. When teachers use assessments and their observations of student behavior to guide instruction, they are using what they know about their students to structure their teaching effectively. Formative assessments may come in many forms. Examples include: pre-tests, preliminary drafts of students' writing, reflection pieces, quizzes, analysis of students' problem-solving techniques, predictions, oral responses to questions posed, or explanations of experimental results. Teachers may also give formative assessments that require students to apply what they are learning in new contexts. For example, the teacher may give students a set of problems that reflect real-world applications related to the big ideas of the unit of study. The object is for the teacher to see which students can solve the problems using the big ideas (or essential concepts) that they have learned. After reviewing the results, students can work in groups to discuss how their solutions were related.

Progress monitoring assessments are ongoing assessments. It is easier to remember what this term means by reversing the two first words and calling it "monitoring progress." These assessments help the teacher determine whether students are learning what is being taught and whether the intervention strategies that are in place for struggling students are effective. They also identify which students are ready to move forward in the curriculum and which students need more background information or intervention techniques. These assessments may be formal or informal, and are often brief. The frequency of their administration may depend on the needs of particular students. An example of a progress monitoring assessment in reading is a running record where teachers individually test students for reading rate and accuracy.

Summative assessments are used to see what students have learned from a unit of study. They reveal the results of instruction and are not necessarily used to guide instruction. They may be in written form, performance-based, project-based, or problem-based. Examples of summative assessments are federal, state, or district assessments, formal culminating presentations, end-of-chapter assessments, unit tests, and end-of-term or semester exams.

Outcome measures are the large-scale assessments that are usually mandated by the government or by school districts. They enable educators to determine the success of individual students, grade levels, subject areas, and/or instructional programs. Outcome assessments may be either norm-referenced or criterion-referenced. Norm-referenced tests compare achievements of students nationally by age or grade level. Examples of norm reference tests are IQ tests and Cognitive Achievement Tests. Criterion-referenced tests measure a student's knowledge of grade-appropriate content or skill. Examples of outcome measurements include physical fitness tests, as well as national and state math and reading tests.

Traditional assessments may be standardized or teacher-created and are usually pencil-and-paper tests. Typically, students are asked to select an answer or recall specific information to complete the assessment. Traditional assessments are used to determine if students have acquired a specific body of knowledge or a particular set of skills taught in the curriculum. Examples of traditional assessments include multiplication quizzes, multiple choice or short answer tests, or an essay that is graded on specific content.

Authentic assessments are usually open-ended and teacher-created. They entail demonstration, construction, performance, experimentation, analysis, synthesis and/or application. They require students to perform tasks that demonstrate that they can meaningfully use their knowledge and skills to solve problems that are rooted in real-world challenges. An example of an authentic assessment is as follows: Students are given a scenario in which they must propose a solution to control the destruction of homes and loss of human life in an area that is frequently plagued by forest fires, hurricanes, tornadoes, or floods. Students must describe the causes of the problem. They must propose a step-by-step solution. They must delineate the costs and benefits of their solution. Finally, they send their proposed solution to the appropriate government officials.

Observing Student Behavior to Inform Instruction

The field of data collection and assessment may seem complex, but much of what you learn about your students will happen naturally in informal ways. Most data, in fact, will be anecdotal. Most teachers already ask their students questions and try to give the necessary background information when students seem lost. However, if you are aware of what to look for when observing students, you can glean an incredible amount of information from carefully listening to and watching what your students say and do. When you become aware of your students' immediate needs, you can become more effective in meeting them.

Just tuning in to your students' conversations, questions, and work habits will give you ideas about how you can help them overcome whatever immediate hurdles they are facing. You can also elicit informal data from students by placing a "wonder box" in your room and encouraging your students to write questions when they are confused or curious. You may ask students to summarize their learning, as you teach, or reflect on their progress. Much of the time you will be able to address your students' concerns in simple ways. You may answer questions, conduct quick reviews or mini-lessons, have conversations to get them on track, get them to help each other, or assist them in finding the materials they need. Sometimes, you may need to use more formal intervention procedures to help them.

The chart on the following two pages lists some student behaviors to look for as you teach. The chart also includes questions that will help guide your observations.

Analysis of Anecdotal Observation of
Students for Teaching Purposes

Area of Anecdotal Observation	Questions to Ask Yourself to Guide Observations	Questions to Ask Yourself to Guide Corrective Action
Quality of student questions	• What do students' questions tell you about their interests and curiosity? • What do students reveal about their confusion through their questions? • Which students ask appropriate questions that will lead them to a deeper understanding of what they are trying to learn, and which students do not? • Which students are reluctant to ask questions?	• How can you address students' areas of interest? • How can you clear their confusion? • How can you help students who need additional encouragement to ask questions?
Quality of student conversations and discussions	• What do students' conversations and discussions reveal about their knowledge, confusions, and interests? • If students are off topic, do they seem to be disinterested? Do they seem to be confused?	• What can you do to help students' focus? • How can you use your students' knowledge to foster deeper understanding? • What can you do to address their areas of confusion? • How can you provide material that interests them?
Content of student answers	• How well do students support their claims when answering questions? • Which students answer questions accurately and completely, and which do not?	• What can you do to help students who are inaccurate, confused, or who do not support claims?

Analysis of Anecdotal Observation of
Students for Teaching Purposes *(cont.)*

Area of Anecdotal Observation	Questions to Ask Yourself to Guide Observations	Questions to Ask Yourself to Guide Corrective Action
Efficiency and accuracy of the methods used to solve problems	• Which students use efficient and accurate problem-solving techniques? Which students do not?	• How can you get students who use effective and accurate methods to share their strategies? • How can you help students who use inaccurate or inefficient techniques to learn new strategies?
Role students take in group projects	• Which students tend to take a leadership position when participating in group work? • Which students sit back and wait for other members of the group to complete work?	• How can you make sure that all students contribute maximally to group projects?
Responsiveness, enthusiasm, and creativity	• Which students are responsive, creative, and enthusiastic about participating in class activities, and which students are not?	• How can you keep responsive students motivated? • How can you motivate students who are reluctant to participate?
Willingness to take intellectual risks	• Which students are confident and are willing to take intellectual risks? Which students are not?	• How can you foster trust and encourage reluctant learners to take risks?
Honesty and openness in self-evaluation	• Which students are aware of problems when they occur and are willing to admit when they are having difficulties? • Which students are unaware or afraid to admit problems?	• How can you encourage students to be honest, open, and reflective in their self-evaluations?
Demeanor when faced with new tasks or assignments	• Which students are eager to tackle new assignments? Which students are reluctant?	• How can you ease the way for reluctant students?

Here is why observational assessment can be helpful. Imagine one of your students is particularly verbal and loves to answer questions out loud. He has a great deal of background knowledge, seems to have a good understanding of topics that are presented orally, and is able to substantiate claims that he makes. However, this student does a minimal amount of work when asked to complete written assignments. His handwriting is almost illegible, he uses only the simplest words, and he makes basic spelling mistakes. He also finds it difficult to focus on any reading assignment, and when given a choice of text, he selects books or articles with large print and lots of pictures. You also notice that he continually rubs his eyes when he is asked to look at something in the front of the room. Because of your observations, you realize that this student may have a problem with his eyesight. After speaking to him, your suspicions are confirmed. You find out that he has glasses but is embarrassed to wear them, and his parents have no idea that he keeps his glasses in his backpack. Now that you know the problem, you are able to help him address it so that he can learn.

One More Thing about Anecdotal Observation

Think about what mechanisms or techniques you will use to gather anecdotal information efficiently. Is it enough to just make mental notes of what you see and hear and try to respond as quickly as possible? If it is impossible to address needs right away, you may want to keep an anecdotal journal and jot down what you notice so that you can respond to it at a later time. There are many applications available on mobile devices which can come in handy for quickly spot checking students and recording observations.

Determining More Formal Assessments to Use

There is much to think about when deciding what additional types of formal assessments to use. You want your assessments to yield as much information as possible about how your students are progressing. The best assessments will not only reveal students' strengths and weaknesses, but will help pinpoint where there is any confusion.

You also need to match the assessments you give to the learning targets that you set. For example, if you want to see how well your students can use their problem-solving skills, you need to give them problems to solve. If you want them to make a considered argument, your assessment should be a venue for that argument. You might have them write a convincing essay or letter, or give a persuasive speech. You may ask them to argue both sides of a controversial issue in a debate, participate in a mock trial, create and perform an advertisement, or write a position paper.

Finally, you will need to determine the criterion for achievement. Specifically, what must your students do to demonstrate success? Students need to know what they are aiming for, so you need to make the criteria that you use to evaluate your students crystal clear to them. Students should be aware of what is expected of them and what constitutes a successful performance or product. There should not be any "gotchas" in education. The goal is for you and the students to get as clear a picture as possible of what needs to be accomplished in the long run and what the next steps might be at any time for meeting the goals.

Evaluating Formative Assessments

It is not necessary to give students a letter or number grade for every assignment or every draft of a paper. However, students need timely feedback. It is helpful to comment on what students can do to improve their work. If you want your students to learn from their mistakes, you must require that they use the feedback you give them. It is also helpful to comment on what your students do well. Nothing builds more on success than success itself.

Evaluating Summative Assessments

Some assessments that you give will be summative, and you will most likely need to evaluate these assessments using a number or letter grading system. Generally, grade books only have spaces for letter or number grades, and most schools require teachers to give report cards to students with letter or number grades on them. Rubrics and checklists for performance assessments can be correlated to letter or number grades if they contain clear criteria for what constitutes success. We examine this in depth in the next chapter.

Conclusion

As you can see, there are many different avenues for collecting information about what your students understand, what they find perplexing, and how well they are reaching the goals of instruction. A well-balanced, varied approach to assessment will provide the clearest picture about your students and will help you accurately and efficiently monitor their progress.

Reflection

1. How do you know what your students are ready to learn, and how can you use this information to make your instruction more effective?

2. Think about your teaching practices. Describe some of the ways that being a student has helped make you a more effective teacher.

3. How can you design assessments that not only reveal your students' strengths and weaknesses, but help you pinpoint where their confusions lie? How can you build in time to address reteaching?

4. What are three ways that you can match your assessments to your specific teaching goals?

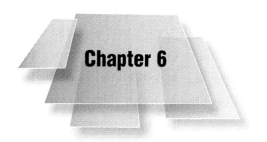

Chapter 6

Choosing and Using the Right Assessments

> *"Data can help to replace hunches and hypotheses with facts concerning what changes are needed."*
>
> —Victoria Bernhardt, 2004

As you develop a unit of study for enduring understanding, you will probably choose a mixture of traditional and authentic assessments for your students. You will also gather much anecdotal data from just watching and listening to what they say and do. As you make decisions about how you will structure their learning, remember that if you are teaching for enduring understanding, the basis of student work must be constructivist. In other words, students need to take an active role and make meaning from what they are investigating. They will need to explore the essential questions of the unit and come to conclusions about the key concepts and principles involved. To do this, they must perform authentic tasks. They must demonstrate that they can transfer their learning to real-world situations. "If assessment is authentic, ongoing, and integrated with classroom instruction, then it is easy to see that it will take many different forms" (Stiggins and Valencia 1997).

Assessment Checklist

In order to make sure that the assessments you choose provide accurate and useful data that can help drive your instruction, it may be useful to use the checklist shown below:

❑	My assessments lead to my final goals for this unit of study.
❑	I have clear learning targets for different points in the unit; I set clear and reasonable benchmarks for student progress along the way.
❑	My assessments reveal student progress; I require students to explain and/or show what they can do in clear, accurate, logical, well-supported, and complete ways.
❑	My assessments help me pinpoint any student confusion.
❑	I have matched the appropriate type of assessment to each student goal. (My assessments include the forms of written work, problem solving, experiments, discussion, and oral presentations that would best demonstrate student progress towards the goals sought.)
❑	My students understand the criteria upon which all of their work will be evaluated.
❑	I have criteria for written work that address content, organization, use of language, and conventions.
❑	I have set criteria for project work that requires students to demonstrate creative and constructivist thinking towards the goals.
❑	I have set criteria for problem solving that requires students to first try to understand the problem and then use efficient and accurate techniques to solve it.
❑	I have set criteria for presentations that address content, organization, and delivery.
❑	I have set criteria for demonstrating understanding that requires students to show that they can transfer their learning to new situations.
❑	I require that students demonstrate that they can accurately assess their own progress and seek help when needed.
❑	I provide clear and specific feedback to students.
❑	I give students the opportunity to use the feedback that they are given to deepen their thinking and improve their performance.
❑	I use the information that I learn from assessing my students to guide my instruction.

Choosing Assessments for the Ecology Unit

We will now revisit each of the learning targets in our ecology unit. Remember that "learning targets" refer to the specific enabling knowledge and enabling skill sets that students will attain because of this unit of study. Our goal is to make sure that the assessments we give are authentic and well-matched to the intent of each learning target. We need to carefully determine which criteria will help us pinpoint the different strengths and needs of our students. We want our assessments to yield as much useful information as possible so we can help our students achieve. This represents Stage Two of Backwards Planning.

The chart on the following page outlines some assessments that can be used to demonstrate how well the students are attaining each learning goal in the ecology unit. It also delineates some very general criteria that may be used to determine the level of student success on each of these assessments. We will look at more specific criteria later in this chapter.

Notice that the ecology unit assessments include a mixture of traditional and authentic assessments. Some assessments require the students to write, while others are performance-based. All assessments require the students to construct meaning, and all of them lead to the learning goals of the unit. Students have some choice in how they wish to demonstrate their understanding, and they do not necessarily have to complete every one of the assessments. The criteria for success are based on how accurately and thoroughly students meet the goals of the assignment.

Stage Two: Determine the Assessment Evidence

Learning Target—Enabling Knowledge (What Students Will Know)	
What renewable natural resources can be used for energy? How can these resources be used?	

Assessment: Design and Build a Biosphere	Criteria for Determining Success
Students will research the requirements of a biosphere, including the species of plants and animals that can survive in one, the symbiotic relationship between them, and the mineral nutrients they need. Students will use small plants such as algae and tiny animals such as crustaceans, water, and airspace to create a biosphere in a sealed glass bottle and record how it works. (Or, students can draw and write an explanation of a projected biosphere.) Present plans in one of the following formats: • report or project • diagram or chart • game • multimedia presentation • explanation or discussion • debate	• sustainability of biosphere (if building a real one); or plausibility of biosphere (if drawing a model) • accuracy and completeness of explanation of all components • substantiation or proof of claims

Learning Target—Enabling Skills (What Students Will Be Able to Do)	
Show how plants and animals provide life-sustaining materials for each other	

Assessment: Design and Build a Biosphere	Criteria for Determining Success
• interview town officials • create a cause-effect diagram	• interview was reported with accuracy • completeness of task • logical implications of problem on the community • practicality of solution • success

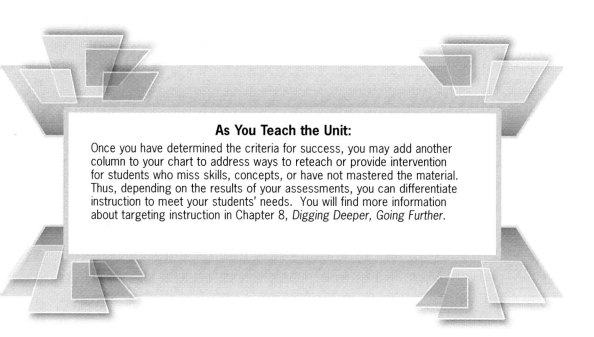

As You Teach the Unit:

Once you have determined the criteria for success, you may add another column to your chart to address ways to reteach or provide intervention for students who miss skills, concepts, or have not mastered the material. Thus, depending on the results of your assessments, you can differentiate instruction to meet your students' needs. You will find more information about targeting instruction in Chapter 8, *Digging Deeper, Going Further.*

Designing Your Own Checklists and Scoring Rubrics

You may wish to design checklists and/or rubrics to evaluate student performances and products. To create either, you would need to establish criteria for what constitutes success or achievement. Students should know exactly how they are going to be evaluated, and they should be given a copy and an explanation of the instrument that will be used. In fact, you may ask your students to co-construct rubrics with you. This has two obvious benefits. First, students have to do the analytical work involved in determining what a successful performance or product would have to include. Also, if they co-construct the rubric, they are invested in the process. Whether or not students help you co-construct the checklist, they should be given a copy of it so that they can evaluate their own work *before* you evaluate it.

Designing Checklists

To design a checklist, you simply list the criteria on which the students should focus for a successful product or performance. The person evaluating the work simply checks off the criteria that are met.

The chart on page 106 shows an example of a story-writing checklist that covers ideas, conventions, grammar, and word usage.

Story Writing Checklist

Story Content and Ideas
❑ the introduction is exciting and makes the reader want to read more
❑ the story has a setting that is important to the plot
❑ the story describes what the characters look like and how they feel
❑ in the beginning, the story describes the build up to the problem
❑ in the middle, the story describes the problem
❑ at the end, the story describes the solution to the problem
Style
❑ sentence type varies (there are statements, questions, etc.)
❑ sentences build upon the ones before them
❑ each paragraph has one main idea
Writing Conventions, Grammar, and Punctuation
❑ handwriting is legible
❑ sentences are complete
❑ correct punctuation is used
❑ first words of sentences, quotations, and all proper nouns are capitalized
Word Usage
❑ colorful words are used
❑ synonyms are used for common words
❑ standard spelling is used

Designing Rubrics

There are two different types of rubrics or rating scales: holistic rubrics and analytic rubrics. We will examine each of these separately.

Holistic Rubrics

In a holistic rubric, you typically evaluate the student's performance or product as a whole. Holistic rubrics are most useful when the emphasis is on a strong completed performance or product, and weakness in one area is not important (Chase 1999). They are generally used for creative assignments where there is no definitive "right answer" (Nikitina 2001). A student's score would simply reflect how well he or she met the major requirements of the assignment. Holistic rubrics are quicker and easier than analytic rubrics to develop and score, but they do not yield a great deal of information. Therefore, they are more often used for summative than for formative evaluations.

A possible template for a holistic rating scale is shown below:

Score	Description of Task Requirements
5	Demonstrates total understanding of the problem. Meets or exceeds all of the task requirements.
4	Demonstrates good or considerable understanding of the problem. All of the task requirements have been included.
3	Demonstrates some or partial understanding of the problem. Most of the task requirements have been included.
2	Demonstrates little understanding of the problem. Some of the task requirements are missing or inaccurate.
1	Attempts to solve problem, but demonstrates no understanding.
0	No response or task not attempted.

Analytic Rubrics

In an analytic rubric, all of the criteria used to evaluate student success on a particular assignment or assessment are delineated. Descriptors explain the evaluation system for each criterion. For example, different descriptors explain what it means to perform at a beginning level, a developing level, an accomplished level, and an exemplary level.

The analytical rubric on pages 109–110 is used to score a magazine article that the students write concerning the ecological problems in their community and the ways that community members can solve those problems. The criteria are based on the *6 + 1 Traits of Writing* (Culham 2003). The descriptors explain what each score means.

When designing this type of rubric, it is important to write the descriptors so that the jumps between criteria are as equal as possible. Normally, the teacher scores each part of the rubric separately and then may add up the scores to get a total. It is possible to translate these scores into letter grades if the teacher chooses a total score range necessary to achieve a particular grade.

Analytic rubrics are more time consuming to construct and to score than holistic rubrics, but they also yield more information. They are useful in making formative evaluations because, "It is possible to create a 'profile' of specific student strengths and weaknesses from analytic rubrics" (Mertler 2001). You can then use this information to target your instruction.

Look at the sample analytic rubric on the following pages. Think about the information that it would give you about each student's writing. How could you use this information to give feedback to students and to target your instruction to their needs?

Sample Analytic Rubric

	(Beginning) 1	(Developing) 2	(Accomplished) 3	(Exemplary) 4	Score
Ideas	Most or all of the ideas are unfocused, inaccurate, unclear or incomplete. There is no attempt to prove or substantiate ideas.	Some of the ideas are inaccurate, unfocused, unclear, or incomplete. There is some attempt to prove or substantiate ideas, but many details are inaccurate, irrelevant, or incomplete.	Most of the ideas are focused, accurate, clear, and complete. Basic proof is given for most of the ideas. Most of the substantiating details are relevant, accurate, and complete.	All of the ideas are focused, clear, accurate, and complete. All of the ideas are substantiated. All of the details are relevant, accurate, and complete.	
Organization	Disorganized. Work does not follow any logical order.	Lacks organization and is sometimes hard to follow. Many sentences do not link to the main message. The conclusion is either missing or inaccurate.	Satisfactorily organized with a logical beginning, middle, and end and is easy to follow. Most sentences link to the main message. The work has an accurate conclusion.	Optimally organized. It has a beginning that hooks the reader. It is easy to follow and all sentences link to the main message. The work has a strong and logical conclusion.	
Voice	Work lacks voice and does not hold the reader's attention.	Beginning attempts at voice. Piece reveals some enthusiasm on the part of the student, but lacks any personal flair.	Some enthusiasm conveyed about the topic. An attempt to give writing a personal flair. The writing evokes some emotion in the reader, and makes the reader want to hear more.	Great enthusiasm conveyed about the topic. The writing has a personal flair. The writing evokes strong emotion in the reader and makes the reader eager to hear more.	

Sample Analytic Rubric *(cont.)*

	(Beginning) 1	(Developing) 2	(Accomplished) 3	(Exemplary) 4	Score
Sentence Fluency	Piece is almost impossible to read and understand. Many sentences begin the same way. Some sentences are choppy, and some sentences are run-ons.	It is possible to read and understand the piece but with some difficulty. There is a beginning attempt to vary sentence type and length.	Piece is easy to read and has some flow. Many sentences vary in length and type. The piece reads fairly smoothly.	Piece is easy to read and understand because it has a natural flow. The sentences vary in length and type. The piece reads in a smooth and seamless way.	
Word Choice	No attempt made to choose words that grab the attention of the reader.	A beginning attempt is made to choose a few strong verbs, colorful phrases, and some precise language, but common words are repeated too often. Piece does not generally grab the attention of the reader because of word choice.	Some strong verbs, colorful phrases, and some precise language are used. Some attempt to avoid repeating common words. Some of the word choices grab the reader's attention.	Many strong verbs, colorful phrases, and precise language are used. Successful use of a variety of interesting words with little repetition of common words and phrases. Words are chosen with obvious care, and they consistently grab the reader's interest and attention.	
Conventions	Little to no use of standard English conventions in piece.	Attempt to use some standard conventions correctly, including punctuation, capitalization, spelling, and grammar, but significant errors interfere with meaning.	Most standard conventions used correctly, including punctuation, capitalization, spelling, and grammar. A few mistakes do not interfere with meaning.	All standard conventions used correctly, including punctuation, capitalization, spelling, and grammar.	

Peer Feedback and Student Self-Reflection

Teachers or other adults are not the only ones that can give constructive feedback to students. In fact, it is vital for students to discuss what they are learning and to give and get feedback from each other. It is also necessary for students to be self-reflective and take responsibility for their own work. These two issues will be addressed separately.

Peer Feedback

In a traditional classroom, a student's audience is typically the teacher. If the teacher is conscientious, he or she reviews the work in detail, makes specific revision and editing comments, and might also offer a grade. Most students will notice the grade, but only give the teacher's comments a cursory glance. If revisions or corrections will result in a higher grade, the student might try to satisfy the teacher by making the suggested corrections. But just how much thought does a student need in order to do this? The comments have been provided to the student in a finished form. Students need to look no further than the teacher's remarks to figure out exactly what to do to improve their grades, and any personal thought about how to improve is absent.

In this model, the teacher did all of the thinking, so the student is unlikely to improve. The teacher was clearly trying to be helpful with all of that careful commenting. But in reality, he or she simply provided the student with a convenient shortcut to avoid thought. That is not our goal. We want our students to take ownership of their work. We want students to revise their work because they care about the final results. To accomplish this, it will take more than having a student do work exclusively for the teacher.

In a learning community, students learn a great deal from each other. In fact, much more learning can take place if the teacher is not the only one giving constructive feedback. Students learn by both giving and receiving feedback. One of the best ways to improve is for students to experience how their peers react to their work.

Truthful feedback is key, and it requires both the trust of the student and the willingness of the peer reviewer to communicate their thoughts honestly and diplomatically. "To respond" comes from the French word *respondere*, which means, "to promise in return." So, response should imply almost a contractual agreement between the students and their respondents. Feedback can be focused on the writing process or on the text itself. Responders can help clarify ideas. However, in the end, the person who does the work owns it, and only he or she can make decisions about how that feedback is to be used.

For peer feedback to be reliable and effective, an organized process needs to be in place in a classroom. This can be a bit tricky. The teacher must structure the process so that students have both the tools and the space to provide meaningful and honest feedback, as well as a safe, nonthreatening way to receive feedback. Interestingly, many students may feel more uncomfortable giving feedback than receiving it. They may not want to appear critical of their friends. Therefore, students need to be taught both the process of giving and receiving constructive feedback. One way to do this is to have students meet in feedback groups.

A possible structure for a feedback group, as outlined on page 113, has four phases, based on a combination of the Liz Lerman Dance Company's *Critical Response Format* (2003), Peter Elbow's *Writing Without Teachers* (1998), and Sondra Perl's work, *Landmark Essays on Writing Process* (1995). These phases include affirmation and observation, questioning the respondents, questioning the student, and criticism and opinions.

Before you begin, tell your students that the structured feedback might seem a little artificial, at first. However, if they "play" along as if it's a game (rather than view it as a restrictive structure) they will soon realize how effective it can be. You can also suggest that after this format has been used for a while, and students are comfortable and are in a position to critique the process, you can revisit it with the class and revise it to best meet their needs.

The process for peer feedback (just like any new process) should first be modeled with the whole class. The teacher should explain the steps involved in constructive feedback and then act as the student who is receiving it. The class follows the process and gives the teacher feedback. Once the teacher has modeled the group feedback structure, and the students understand the process, the teacher should form feedback groups. Feedback groups work best with three to six students, and it is helpful to keep the same group together so that students have the time to form a trusting relationship with each other. When the groups meet, the teacher should circulate and sit in on different groups to help the process run smoothly and effectively.

The aim of peer review is to help as many students as possible, so students should take turns going through the entire process. It is helpful if all students in the group have a copy of the text that they are analyzing so that they can take notes.

Phases of Peer Review and Feedback

Phase 1: Affirmation and Observation
❑ present work and any necessary background information
❑ respondents offer positive remarks
❑ respondents retell what they heard
Phase 2: Question the Responders
❑ ask for specific feedback
Phase 3: Respondents Question the Student
❑ ask clarifying questions
❑ offer constructive criticism
❑ offer reflective statements
Phase 4: Criticism and Opinions
❑ student asks for suggestions
❑ respondents give suggestions

Student Self-Reflection

Another way to help students take responsibility for their work is to foster self-reflection. For honest self-reflection to take place, students must feel a sense of trust. Students must feel secure that if they expose their confusions or admit to having problems understanding something, they will get help and not be ridiculed. According to Tileston (2004), students' brains change focus when they perceive a threat. The brain stem actually takes over and directs behavior when a person feels threatened: "When threat is perceived, excessive cortisol (a hormone) is released into the body, causing high-order thinking to take a backseat to automatic functions that may help you survive." In terms of self-reflection, students cannot learn to see potential if they think their ideas will be "laughed at or put down." They fear "embarrassment in front of peers," they feel disrespected or isolated, or they do not have the "adequate tools, time, or resources to carry out assignments" (Tileston 2004). The teacher must give the clear message to the class that they are all part of a learning community, and that their job is to help each other. The idea is not to parade perfection but to fully examine what is confusing, difficult, and messy in order to deepen both thought and understanding.

You may ask students to keep reflection logs or fill out personal or group evaluation sheets that detail what they are doing, how productively or effectively they are learning, what problems or confusions they are encountering, why they are experiencing these problems, and how they think they can work more effectively. You may meet with individual students and confer with them about their self-reflections and make suggestions for improvement. You may also ask students to help each other with problems or to share their reflections, ideas, and problem solving strategies with the class. It is essential that you continually give students the message that we are all trying to help each other. A healthy message is that mistakes just pose challenges for us to find new and better ways of doing things.

Conclusion

The fundamental purpose of assessment is to enable us to target instruction in order to effectively meet our students' needs. To do this, we must make sure that we actually test what we want our students to know and that the criteria we use to evaluate them yields clear information about how we can best assist them. Students need timely and specific feedback to improve the quality of their thinking and their work. Students can also give each other valuable feedback if they are taught constructive methods for doing so.

Reflection

1. How can the Assessment Checklist help you evaluate student performance? What is one specific assessment you might use that would give you the information you need about student achievement of a particular goal?

2. Checklists and rubrics have somewhat different uses. How can you effectively use checklists and/or scoring rubrics to evaluate student performance? How can you convert these to grades, if necessary?

3. What systems can you put in place so that your students can give and receive regular, effective peer feedback? What can you put in place so that your students become self-reflective and can honestly evaluate their own work?

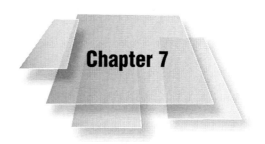

Chapter 7

Developing Effective and Engaging Daily Lesson Plans

I hear, and I forget.
I see, and I remember.
I do, and I understand.

—Chinese Proverb

O nce you know the goals that you are seeking and have determined the types of assessments that will give you the clearest information on how well your students are doing, it is time to plan your daily lessons and activities. Remember, you must always keep your end goals in mind as you plan.

In this chapter, we examine the following:

- steps involved in reaching informative goals

- steps involved in reaching procedural goals

- specific ways for making daily lesson plans effective and engaging

- a checklist of things to think about as you prepare your own daily lessons

- ways of helping reluctant students become engaged learners

Prioritizing

In order to make the best use of the time that you have for your unit of study, begin by blocking out the entire unit on a rough calendar. This will include an estimate of the time you will spend introducing the topic and explaining the essential questions that the students will explore. It will also include the approximate time frame your students will need to reach the different learning targets. The calendar will end with your culminating activity. You may use a variation of the Sample Unit Overview Grid for the Ecology Unit (Appendix D, page 164) as a guide.

There are several things to keep in mind as you block out your unit. You need to teach concepts in a coherent way that will ultimately lead to the results which you are seeking. First, prioritize what you want the students to learn. Remember that the concepts presented must build upon each other. Therefore, you need to consider the most logical order for teaching. Think about the inherent difficulty of the topics your students will explore. Which ones will probably be easy for students to grasp, and which ones might be difficult? Then think about the particular students that you are teaching. What background information do your students have about the topic, what skills do they already possess, and where are they struggling? Finally, formulate your best approximation of the time frame involved in meeting the different goals of the unit. You will most likely have to make changes as you proceed. You need to be flexible so that you can target instruction based on what your assessments reveal. However, an estimated overview of the unit is useful to help you structure your daily activities.

Once you have an estimated time frame in mind, you will need to carefully plan your daily lessons and activities around the specific learning targets. How will you most effectively address each objective in your daily lessons? How will you structure your lessons so that your students are actively engaged? What types of activities will help your students construct meaning from what they do? How can you help students understand the big ideas and organize the facts they learn around these ideas? And remember, since the ultimate goal is to teach students to be able to use what they learn beyond the classroom, you should include activities that will give students practice applying what they learn in a wider context.

Informational Versus Procedural Goals

We will now examine the types of lessons that are designed to help students meet knowledge and procedural learning targets. In her book, *What Every Teacher Should Know about Instructional Planning* (2004), Donna Tileston refers to the knowledge or critical information that students must have (the facts, dates, names, events, steps, formulas, and vocabulary) as *declarative objectives*. (It is what we called our Knowledge Learning Targets.) Tileston uses the term *procedural objectives* for the strategies and steps that students need to be able to use to perform different operations. (This is what we referred to as our Procedural Learning Targets). Tileston explains that often students need to learn declarative information before they learn procedural information because students need to understand basic facts before they can do something with them. For example, in our ecology unit, students would need to know the conditions and elements that animals and plants need to live and what life-sustaining materials they can provide for each other before they would be able to create a viable biosphere.

However, the fact that students need to have critical and accurate information to perform specific procedures does not mean that teachers need to divide the unit into two distinct parts. Students do not need to first learn all of the information that pertains to the unit and then learn all of the procedures involved in applying that information. What is important is that students know the information and concepts necessary to understand and perform particular procedures as they come up. To illustrate this, let's revisit an example from our ecology unit.

Suppose students are asked to build a viable biosphere. To do this, they need to understand some basic facts, such as which species of plants and animals can survive in the biosphere, the symbiotic relationships between the organisms in the biosphere, and the different nutrients that the organisms need. Without these facts, students will not be able to complete the assignment successfully.

Declarative Objectives: Addressing What Students Must Know

Helping your students meet their informational goals and helping them meet procedural goals require somewhat different strategies. Tileston describes how each may be best addressed in daily lesson plans. She outlines a specific three-phase process for students to effectively understand, store, and retrieve information, and a different three-phase process to learn how to perform procedures accurately and efficiently (Tileston 2004).

Here are the three phases of knowledge acquisition:

- Phase 1: Make meaning from information

- Phase 2: Organize the information

- Phase 3: Store the information for later use

In the chart on the following pages, the left-hand column lists what students must do to process, organize, and store critical information for later use. The right-hand column explains effective teaching strategies for helping students do each of these things. As you develop your daily lessons, you can use this chart to select the strategies that are most relevant for what you are teaching.

Typically, questions that begin with the words *what, where, when,* and *why* elicit factual answers. If you ask students to justify, substantiate, validate, corroborate, support, authenticate, explain, clarify, or prove their answers, it usually leads them to a more in-depth explanation of the facts.

Declarative Objectives:
Addressing What Students Must Know

Knowledge Acquisition	Strategies to Help Students
Phase 1: Make Meaning from Information	• **Explain to students the goals that you are seeking** and how learning this information will help them meet these goals. This provides a reason for students to attend to the information. • **Help students make personal connections** to the information. Show them how the information relates to their lives through a story or poem, or by discussing what they might do if faced with a similar choice or dilemma. • **Help students access their background knowledge** and experiences. This provides a personal context for receiving new information. It also provides a way to help students connect their new learning to what they have previously learned. • **Enrich the context so that students can receive and connect new information.** Tell stories around the information and have students examine it from different points of view. Discuss and demonstrate its relevance. This activates memory systems in different parts of the brain. • **Intersperse facts, concepts, and anecdotes** so that several different neuron systems in the brain can remain activated and students can make meaningful connections. • **Provide activities in which students can use all of their senses when learning the information.** This will also activate their different memory pathways and facilitate making associations. • **Encourage students to ask questions** about concepts or information that confuses them or piques their curiosity. This will help them understand the new material and make significant associations.

Declarative Objectives:
Addressing What Students Must Know *(cont.)*

Knowledge Acquisition	Strategies to Help Students
Phase 2: Organize the Information	• **Help students build, reflect on, and discuss connections** they make as they look at new information. This will help students see patterns and organize the information that they are learning. • **Help students determine what is important and what is not.** Have students discuss or note information that is logical, connected, or which proves or disproves a point. Help students think about which information substantiates or negates a claim. Have them detect and discuss which information seems irrelevant and/or confusing and why. Have them examine conflicting or controversial claims to discern the slant of the author. • **Help students organize information into what Tileston (2004) calls "linguistic and/or nonlinguistic formats."** Help them organize information linguistically by having them summarize, outline, write journal entries or reflection pieces, or by having them discuss it. Have students organize information in a nonlinguistic format through the use of timelines, graphs, or charts. • **Provide or have students create graphic organizers** such as Venn diagrams, story maps, flow charts, or cause/effect charts. This will help students visualize the information. • **Help students organize their written work and their notebooks so that new information is connected in logical ways.** This will help them form a conceptual understanding of the new content and will give them a tool to later review the information in ways that make sense.
Phase 3: Store the Information for Later Use	• **Use music, movement, symbols, emotional connections, and colors, (whenever possible) to activate the different memory systems** in the brain so that they can work together to help students remember and later retrieve the information readily, accurately, and appropriately. • **Show students how they can transfer information or procedures and have them practice doing it.** In other words, have students apply what they are learning in order to make new connections or solve new problems. You can do this by first showing students how, when, where, and why this information can be used. Then give students plenty of time to practice applying what they know in new circumstances. • **Have students reflect on their learning through logs, journals, debates, discussions, and conversations.** Have students discuss patterns of the information that they are learning. This will help construct meaning, make connections, and store information in long-term memory.

Procedural Learning Targets: Addressing What Students Must Be Able to Do

We now look at some strategies for helping students learn procedural information. The chart on pages 125–126 details what students must do to use or apply information, and it includes ideas on how teachers can most effectively help students address procedural objectives. This is also a three-phase process. However, before looking at this chart, we will examine several different types of strategies that people commonly use to solve different types of problems.

According to Marzano (1992), there are three basic types of strategic approaches that people use to solve problems. It is important to be able to distinguish between them. The first approach is following a specific set of steps, or an algorithm, to solve a problem or achieve a goal, such as a step-by-step procedure to solve a long division problem. Algorithms are reliable. If you follow the algorithm exactly, you will always get the same result.

A second approach is using tactics or general rules, such as learning how to read a geological survey map by understanding the rules by which it was created. Each time you look at the map, you may notice a fresh nuance.

The third approach is using strategies, or universal ways, to approach a task, such as using the scientific method when conducting an experiment. Strategies are more general than algorithms or tactics, and different people using the same strategy often get different results. According to Tileston (2004), "Teaching students the tactics, algorithms, and strategies used in procedural knowledge is valuable not just in the classroom, but for life."

Eric Jensen (1998) explained that students need challenging problems to solve, but problem solving isn't limited to one area of the brain. Different parts of the brain or neural pathways are involved because students can solve problems in different ways. You can solve a problem through constructing a model, through the use of pen and paper, through statistics, through discussion, through debate, through artwork, or through demonstration. "That means it is critical to expose students to a variety of approaches to solving problems" (1998). However, if you are aware of the types of procedures (algorithms, tactics, or strategies) that are most effectively used to solve a specific problem, you will be more likely to be able to structure your teaching in an optimal way.

Questions that begin with *how* typically require procedural knowledge. Asking students to build, construct, create, demonstrate, express, put together, display, exhibit, use, figure out, apply, prove, decipher, or solve something requires them to show you the depth of their procedural knowledge.

Now let's take a look at some instructional strategies useful for helping students reach procedural objectives. The following chart on pages 125–126 outlines Tileston's three phases for attaining procedural goals, and some strategies that teachers can use to help students do this effectively. Again, you should just select the strategies that you think fit best in terms of what you are teaching.

Here are the three phases of attaining procedural goals:

- Phase 1: Construct mental models
- Phase 2: Shape the information to own it
- Phase 3: Internalize procedures for automaticity

Procedural Goals:
Addressing What Students Must Be Able to Do

Attaining Procedural Goals	Strategies to Help Students
Phase 1: Construct Mental Models	• **Help students access their background knowledge and connect** new skills, strategies, or procedures to previously learned ones. • **Explain the general principles** involved in using the procedure or process. • **Model how you use the procedure or process.** Think aloud as you demonstrate it. This helps students see how the strategy is used and provides a model for them to talk through their own problems. • **Work with students to write steps, construct examples, or create flow charts to solve problems.** Include the reasons for each step. This helps students think through the steps, understand the purpose behind them, and provides a visual aid for solving problems. • **Help students mentally rehearse procedures.** This helps them understand and remember the logical steps involved in solving problems.
Phase 2: Shape the Information to Own It	• **Explain to students that each person is unique and each needs to internalize them and make the processes their own.** Students must understand the reasons for the steps involved and think through the most effective and efficient ways to proceed. • **Explain possible pitfalls or common errors** when using specific procedures. • **Have students brainstorm and discuss alternate ways** of solving problems. • **Give students lots of time to practice procedures** in different contexts and circumstances including alternate ways of approaching the problem. • **Have students reflect on the procedures** as they use them. Have them explain what is working and what is not. Ask them what modifications they might make to improve efficiency and accuracy. Then have them use their modified procedures and reflect on the results. • **Have students discuss their progress** and continually reflect on what they are learning. • **Provide ongoing feedback** to students, and teach them how to provide effective feedback for each other.

Procedural Goals:
Addressing What Students Must Be Able to Do (cont.)

Attaining Procedural Goals	Strategies to Help Students
Phase 3: Internalize Procedures for Automaticity	• **Give students plenty of ways to practice** and plenty of time to practice. • **Let students first use the modalities with which they are most comfortable** (visual, auditory, or kinesthetic) to reinforce what they are learning. Different students may need to hear or discuss their new learning. Others learn best when they draw a representation, build a model, or perform. • **Help students transfer what they know by providing new problems.** Have students apply what they know in new circumstances. • **Have students discuss and chart their progress.** • **Have students use a checklist or rubric against which they can evaluate their progress.** Have them make the necessary changes as they go. • **Have students set new goals** for themselves.

Choosing Effective and Engaging Daily Learning Activities

In planning your daily lessons, it is you who must determine which instructional practices will be most effective in helping your students to make appropriate connections, understand the underlying principles or the big ideas of the unit, and apply what they are learning to solve new problems.

According to Wiggins and McTighe (1998; 2005), in order to design "a good plan for learning, in light of goals," the activities you give students must be both "engaging and effective." Wiggins and McTighe define an engaging lesson as one that draws all the diverse learners in your classroom into the subject or topic "by the nature of the demands, mystery, or challenge," of the assignment or activity that they are expected to complete. This does not mean that assignments are structured so that learners merely enjoy the work, but that they are "worthy of their intellect, centered on big ideas and [contain] important performance challenges." Wiggins and McTighe define effective activities as ones that make the learner more "competent and productive at worthy work."

For lessons to be both effective and engaging, the big picture must be clear to the students throughout the unit of study. Activites should lead to the goals of instruction. They should be hands-on, rooted in interesting real-world applications, and challenge students in a safe but meaningful way. Since different students have diverse strengths and needs, there should be more than one way for students to demonstrate their understanding. Students must also know what is expected of them, be able to monitor their own progress, get specific and timely feedback, and learn from their mistakes. Students should be asked to do things that truly matter.

As you plan your daily lessons, you may find it useful to use the checklist on the next page.

Instructional Planning Checklist

❏ Lesson objectives are aligned to national, state and/or local standards.

❏ Objectives are posted for all students to see, and are referred to throughout the lesson (or unit of study).

❏ The lesson is based on the needs of students.

❏ The lesson is designed to help students attain the knowledge and skills outlined in their learning targets.

❏ The activities are engaging and effective.

❏ Expectations for students are clear.

❏ Desired results for the lesson are clearly stated.

❏ What students need to know and understand (critical content or declarative knowledge) is addressed.

❏ What students need to be able to do (procedural knowledge) is addressed.

❏ Strategies are designed to help students acquire the declarative or procedural knowledge.

❏ Students have the necessary tools, resources, knowledge, and experiences to be successful.

❏ The lesson follows the Gradual Release of Responsibility model (as follows):

- Teacher demonstrates the importance of the information.
- Teacher models the new skill or strategy and thinks aloud while showing students what to do.
- Teacher gives students the opportunity to practice with guidance so students have time to make meaning, understand connections, reflect on their learning, get feedback, deepen thought, and make any necessary changes.
- Students work independently to apply (or transfer) learning to new situations.
- Students reflect on their independent work, ask questions, share their findings, give each other feedback, and make any necessary revisions.

❏ Conference time is planned to answer students' questions and clear up confusions.

❏ Students' strengths and weaknesses are understood, both from anecdotal data and from formal and informal assessment data.

❏ Students give evidence that they are reflective and critical thinkers, articulate communicators, and skilled problem solvers.

❏ Assessment data helps target instruction to student needs, instruction is scaffolded (as follows):

- mini-lessons and practice, leveled resources and materials, modified assignments when necessary, and continual feedback for struggling students
- enrichment, compacting, or advanced material for students who already know the material
- support for English language learners

Encouraging the Passive Learner

Many students are comfortable being passive learners. Even students who prefer active learning may be so accustomed to merely memorizing information to get good grades that they find it daunting to do anything else. The question is, how can you help shift the paradigm from a teacher-centered classroom to one that is learning-centered? You will need to guide students through this change of focus. How can you light the fire of curiosity in passive students, motivate them to focus on the learning process, and take responsibility for their own learning? There is no one simple answer to this problem, but there are several key ideas that can help you do this.

First, it is important to foster a learning environment in which students feel comfortable exploring material, asking questions, actively investigating ideas, and monitoring their own progress. Your students need to know that this is what you value most in your classroom. You must emphasize to your students that they will learn best when they take responsibility for their work. Let them know that you want them to seek understanding. You need to assure students that their questions and ideas are vital, that their mistakes will lead to further inquiry and learning, and that they will learn from each other as well as from you.

Certain teaching methods promote active learning, and there are specific techniques that you can use to help reluctant students be more open. For example, discussion is preferred over lecture for promoting critical thinking and engagement. During class discussions, you need to be observant and note which students are least likely to respond. You then have several options. You can divide your class into discussion groups so that students who are shy in a whole class setting might feel more comfortable about responding. You can encourage your passive learners to respond by speaking with them privately about what you can do to ease the way for them. You may pose specific questions that are designed to draw out a particular student or ask questions that tap the knowledge of different students on different skill levels. You need to be careful about embarrassing shy students.

Engaging and Effective Instruction

Wiggins and McTighe (2005) have asked different groups of teachers across the educational spectrum (from first year to veterans and from kindergarten to college), to respond to two types of questions: Which factors affect student engagement and which factors impact learning effectiveness? The results they received were fascinating.

According to these teachers, learners are most *engaged* in school when the assigned work has the following attributes:

- hands-on

- involves mysteries or problems

- provides variety

- offers opportunity to adapt, modify, or somehow personalize the challenge

- balances cooperation and competition [between] self and others

- is built upon a real world or meaningful challenge

- uses provocative interactive approaches such as case studies, mock trials, and other kinds of simulated challenges

- involves real audiences or other forms of "authentic" accountability of results

Teachers typically responded that effective learning has the following attributes:

- work is focused on clear and worthy goals

- students understand the purpose and the rationale for the work

- models and exemplars are provided

- clear public criteria allow students to accurately monitor their progress

- there is a limited fear and maximal incentive to try hard, take risks, and learn from mistakes without penalty

- the ideas are made clear by linking students' experiences to the world beyond

- opportunities are provided to self-assess and self-adjust based on feedback

When my sister was in high school, she was very self-conscious. She was a conscientious student but was afraid to raise her hand and speak out in class. One day, she got up her nerve and raised her hand. My sister was traumatized when the teacher remarked, "Well, isn't it amazing. Helen wants to answer the question!" My sister told me she never raised her hand in high school again.

You may encourage shy or passive learners to participate in class discussions. You can promote this both by the types of questions you ask and by the structure provided for students to answer them. You should give all students time to reflect on and rehearse their thoughts and ideas before responding orally. This can be done in a variety of ways. You may have students use reflection logs where they write their responses to questions or to ideas before they respond out loud. You can also have them rehearse their ideas by having them first turn and talk to a partner before opening up a class discussion. This forces even the most passive learner to take part in class discussions.

Try gearing questions to specific learners. Narrow questions or add context for students with less knowledge about a topic and open the questions up for students with more knowledge. If you know that a student can contribute something relevant to the class discussion because of a special talent or cultural practice, ask that student specifically about it. A particularly shy student might appreciate an opportunity to privately rehearse in advance. You can explicitly direct appropriate questions to specific students. The most important thing is that you validate your students so that they feel good about contributing and will be willing to do it again. Make sure that you do not embarrass students who answer questions incorrectly.

Helping Class Discussion Flow

To help a class discussion flow more naturally, you might allow your students to respond to each other directly. If you do this with your whole class, it is helpful if the furniture is arranged so that the students can see each other's faces. You can also have a small group of students demonstrate a good discussion using a fishbowl technique. In this model, a small group of students sit near each other and discuss a topic while the rest of the class listens in. In an open fishbowl model, a few extra seats are placed in the fishbowl. Other students (and even the teacher) can join in when they have a comment or question to contribute and then go back to their regular seats when they are through.

You can also structure class discussions so that you have a better idea of who to call on next. I worked with a teacher in New Jersey whose second grade students developed different hand signals to show when they wanted to make a connection to something said, add something, make an inference, or ask a question. The students came up with both the idea of making signals and the signals themselves. The teacher told me that it was great because she had a better idea of who to call on next to keep a class conversation flowing. Sometimes she let the child who was speaking decide who to call on next.

Learning Styles

In planning your daily lessons, it is also important to remember that students have different learning styles and preferences and thus have different ways of responding to new material. Encouraging students to examine their learning styles will help them develop better learning strategies. One of the ways to do this is to administer and discuss the implications of a learning style inventory. Students also become more actively involved when they are allowed to make some of the choices. You can provide some activities that will give students more control over how they learn and how they can demonstrate what they have accomplished. Students can demonstrate their knowledge through constructing models, performing experiments, writing reports, solving problems, participating in presentations, etc.

However, to be effective on a daily basis, the most important thing you can do is to remain flexible and responsive. If you open your classroom up to student thought and inquiry, your room will become a community where all members can learn from each other. If your students see that you value their ideas and their curiosity, and that they are safe from being judged, they will be encouraged to learn actively. If you make it clear that you realize your students have unique strengths and needs, you will be able to target your instruction effectively. You do not have to be perfect, but if you think flexibly, you will have the best chance of successfully meeting the challenges that a student-centered classroom will undoubtedly pose. And your students will have the best chance of reaping its enormous benefits.

Conclusion

Students need to take ownership of their learning. Encourage all of them to explore new concepts, construct meaning, take intellectual risks, and learn from their mistakes. Structure class discussions so that the more reluctant students become more comfortable and so there is a natural flow of ideas. Understanding students' learning styles and preferences will also help you plan effectively. Above all, if you remain flexible and responsive to students' needs and they know that you respect them and value their ideas and opinions, they will take ownership of their learning.

Reflection

1. Define engaging and effective learning. When is your teaching most effective? When is it most engaging?

2. Are there any principles you can generalize about making instruction effective and engaging?

3. What are some procedural expectations you have for students? What are your informational learning targets? How can you effectively plan lessons around specific learning targets?

4. How do you encourage the most passive, reluctant, or resistant learners in your classroom? Is your room environment conducive to an active learning experience?

5. How can you get your classroom discussions to flow more smoothly? How can you get your students to take greater responsibility for their own learning?

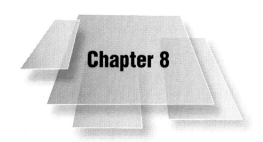

Chapter 8

Digging Deeper, Going Further

> *"What we share in common makes us human. How we differ makes us individuals. In a classroom with little or no differentiated instruction, only student similarities seem to take center stage. In a differentiated classroom, commonalities are acknowledged and built upon, and student differences become important elements in teaching and learning as well."*
>
> —Carol Ann Tomlinson, 1995

Differentiating Units of Study to Meet the Global Challenge

According to the Department of Education, the official mission of schools in the United States is "to promote student achievement and preparation for global competitiveness by fostering educational excellence and ensuring equal access" (2001–2009). This is a lofty goal, and one that is obviously difficult to achieve. It requires deep thought about two overarching and essential questions. The first question encompasses the "what" of education. What tools will students likely need to successfully compete in an increasingly complex world? If we are to prepare our students well for the world beyond school, we need to have an understanding of what they will need to know and be able to do in the future. The second question encompasses the "how" of education, and is equally important: How can we best meet the diverse needs of our students? In this chapter, we examine each of these issues separately, focusing on how to design lessons and units of study that prepare all of our students for the future through the use of effective and practical differentiation techniques.

Preparing Students for the Future

It is impossible to specifically know what students will need in order to successfully compete in the future. However, we know one thing for certain: The world is continually and rapidly changing. New technologies are revolutionizing the world as we know it and connecting people in ways that would have been unimaginable just a few years ago. Old jobs are disappearing and new ones are popping up at an amazing rate. As Karl Fisch and Scott McLeod so aptly stated on their TeacherTube video, *Did You Know?/Shift Happens*: "We are currently preparing students for jobs that don't yet exist / using technologies that haven't yet been invented / in order to solve problems that we don't even know are problems yet" (http://www.youtube.com). Talk about a global challenge!

However, the fact that the world is changing so rapidly provides us with important clues about what we need to concentrate on in our schools. Although we have no crystal ball to reveal the mysteries of the future, we do know that we will have to prepare our students to meet the new challenges which they will undoubtedly have to face. We know for sure that our students will eventually enter an ever-changing and complex world, where at the minimum, they will need to do the following:

- read with understanding
- communicate their ideas with clarity
- make appropriate connections
- distinguish between reliable and unreliable sources of information
- investigate information accurately and efficiently
- make decisions based on sound reasoning

- think through new problems
- apply what they know to solve these problems

Thus, if we are to prepare all of our students for the future, the essential goals of education remain the same for every child. We need to help promote deep and accurate thinking about the big ideas at the heart of subjects we teach. We also need to show our students how to apply their knowledge to solve new problems. As we have discussed in the previous chapters, this can be best accomplished by carefully structuring units of study. Students need to investigate and construct meaning about important issues and then demonstrate their understanding through their own products, presentations, and problem solving. But a vexing question remains: How can we help students with different needs achieve the same big goals?

The Need for Differentiation

More than ever before, schools serve children from an enormous variety of ethnic, cultural, family, language, and socioeconomic backgrounds. Students enter schools with diverse readiness levels, skills, interests, strengths, needs, motivations, and learning styles. Our students may also come from families that run the gamut when it comes to expectations for formal academic learning. On one extreme are the families who consider education to be the key to all future accomplishments and who expect their children to perform perfectly in school at all times. Some of these parents take on their children's responsibilities in order to protect them from making mistakes. They may become overly involved in every aspect of school. On the other extreme are families who have had unsatisfactory experiences in school themselves. They may have no real expectation that schools will improve the lives of their children. Some of these families are simply overwhelmed by the daily struggle to survive, and may not have the skills necessary to help at home. These parents may provide little to no support when it comes to academic endeavors. Then there are all of the families in between. Yet, as educators, we are equally responsible for all of these students in our charge.

One thing is certain. The rich diversity of families we serve necessitates an overhaul of the traditional, one-size-fits-all instructional model. All students need an appropriate amount of challenge to prevent them from becoming either overwhelmed or bored. Too much challenge can cause anxiety, withdrawal, and even despair. Too little challenge can cause tedium and wasted student potential. This is a tremendous responsibility for educators, especially because problems that are not attended to in a timely manner can easily escalate.

Consider the following challenges of typical schools: Schools must support large numbers of both academically marginal students, as well as students who are English language learners with limited resources. Students who experience minor difficulties often do not receive timely intervention. As these students fall further behind, their problems are compounded and ultimately, become overwhelming.

At the same time, schools must meet the needs of on-level, above-level, and gifted students. Too often, more advanced students feel bored by the repetition that is all too common in the typical classroom and they may become unmotivated. Since these students generally test well no matter what their schools do, their special needs can be (and too often are) ignored, resulting in a tragic loss of potential.

To help all of our diverse students reach the goals of education, we must target the instructional methods and materials we use so that we can meet their varying needs. Differentiated instruction occurs when teachers provide instruction that is tailored to meet the differences among learners.

As Diane Leipzig (2000) explained, differentiation is not just about having different students do different things. Teachers must continually assess the understanding and progress of their students. They must vary instruction in order to create the optimal learning experiences based on their students' changing needs. According to Carol Ann Tomlinson and Jay McTighe (2006), "Differentiated instruction offers a framework for addressing learner variance as a critical component of instructional planning." A teacher needs to create many paths to learning. Differentiating instruction is not a simple process, but it is critical for success.

Connecting Differentiated Instruction to Backwards Planning

The book *Integrating Differentiated Instruction and Understanding by Design* (2006), coauthored by Carol Ann Tomlinson and Jay McTighe, explores how to incorporate differentiation strategies when designing units of study. According to these authors, Backwards Planning and differentiated instruction go hand in hand. Backwards Planning primarily focuses on determining what is essential for all students to learn and what assessment evidence we must collect as proof of that learning. All students (from those who struggle, to the most advanced) need to have curricula that lead to enduring understandings of the big ideas that are at the heart of a unit of study. All students need guidance and support to help them develop their thought processes. All students learn best if they engage in deep thinking. Differentiated instruction supports this process by meeting every students' needs.

Our goal as teachers should be to maximize the difference that we can make in the lives of the students in our charge by engaging them in deep thinking. This requires that we understand a number of specific strategies and techniques that we can use to differentiate daily lessons based on students' needs, interests, and learning styles.

You can plan units of study based on Backwards Planning principles that include differentiation techniques using the Backwards Planning template, outlined in Appendix C, page 163. The following is a checklist of things you may include in your Backwards Planning approach in order to ensure that all students reach the same goals and that the assignments are scaffolded and differentiated to meet their needs. The pages that follow also list some of the materials and resources that you may wish to use for scaffolding and differentiating instruction. You do not have to include everything that is listed here—these are just helpful ideas.

Stage One: Identify Desired Results

The elements in this stage are identical for every student because the goal of instruction is to help every student understand the big ideas and underlying principles of the topics that they are studying.

- ❑ enduring understandings, essential questions, and big ideas at the heart of the unit of study
- ❑ learning targets that delineate what students will know, understand, and be able to do as a result of the unit of study
- ❑ culminating project or performance assessment that will demonstrate each student's deep understanding of the topic

Stage Two: Determine the Assessment Evidence

This is the pivotal stage for differentiating instruction: You determine which assessments are likely to give you the most specific information about the progress of each student.

- ❑ pre-assessments based on identified outcomes (these might include surveys of pre-existing knowledge or ideas about the topic to be studied)
- ❑ formative assessments, both formal and informal (these should be designed to determine the level of student mastery for each learning target and should pinpoint any instructional needs)
- ❑ several forms of assessments/assignments that contain the same concepts (some students may need additional help or resources to complete an assessment or assignment)
- ❑ assessment activities that give students some choice in how to demonstrate understanding.
- ❑ observation checklists (what do you notice that your students do well or need help doing?)
- ❑ student self-reflection/evaluation sheets
- ❑ class, group, and individual record-keeping sheets
- ❑ differentiated rubrics with specific descriptors to ensure quality

It is not helpful to write all of your daily lessons in advance. Use data from your assessments and your observations of student behavior to plan effective daily learning experiences *as* you teach the unit. Some of the strategies listed in this checklist may be unfamiliar to you; refer to Appendices E, F, and G (pages 165–169) for further explanation on differentiating instruction.

- ❏ lessons that are differentiated by content, process, and/or product based on student skill level, interests, and/or learning styles
- ❏ tiered assignments with resources and materials at different readability levels, levels of complexity, and levels of abstraction
- ❏ flexible grouping (small and large group) based on student skills, interests, and/or learning preferences
- ❏ ideas for teaching the same concepts in multiple ways, geared to using different modalities, multiple intelligences, and learning preferences
- ❏ differentiated questioning techniques
- ❏ ideas for compacting or enriching curricula for advanced students
- ❏ peer coaching activities
- ❏ large group, small group, and independent investigation activities
- ❏ student contracts and self-paced activities
- ❏ activity choices based on student interests
- ❏ inquiry-based and open-ended assignments
- ❏ small and large group discussion/debate topics

Use Differentiated Materials and Resources

Use the following guidelines to help you organize in advance to differentiate instruction:

- Find texts and other resources that cover the same concepts but at different readability levels.
- Use graphic organizers that provide different levels of scaffolding.
- Employ "sense-making" activities for students with specific needs, such as word banks, illustrations, video clips, thesauruses, picture dictionaries, etc.
- Include vocabulary development activities for English language learners and English speaking students.
- Provide leveled anchor activities that students can do when they finish their assigned work (these should include interesting options designed to help students explore and extend the big ideas of the topic).
- Compact the curriculum for advanced learners.
- Assign several alternative homework activities to afford more choice.

Everyday Examples of Differentiation:
Don't Forget Your High-Achievers!

I have three family tales to tell that brought home the need for differentiation.

- When my daughter was in third grade, she was a very quiet student. She did her work easily, but because she was very shy, her teachers didn't know much about her. That year she was in a "team" taught classroom. One of her teachers was puzzled about how my daughter solved math problems. According to the teacher, my daughter always ended up with the right answers, but drew seemingly unrelated pictures as she did her work. The teacher couldn't figure out why my daughter did this and asked me to find out. When I questioned my daughter, she smiled, begged me not to tell her teacher, and said, "I do that because I don't want to hand in the work before other students. If I do, the teacher will just give me another sheet of problems to do!"

- On the other hand, my son found out what could happen if you ask the teacher the wrong question. When he was in seventh grade, his science teacher complained to me that he had embarrassed her in front of the whole class about a month before, and that she had sent him to the guidance counselor. I was unnerved by the teacher's story—my son had never mentioned the incident, so I felt unprepared. I braced myself as the teacher began to explain what happened. She had explained to the class that a physical property was one that you could see, touch, or feel. My son had the "audacity" to raise his hand and ask, "What about microscopic properties, can't they be physical?" The teacher was convinced that he had asked this question just to make her look foolish. Then, she unleashed a litany of complaints against my son. He never raised his hand again; he knew everything already; he was always looking out the window. By this time, I could feel my own face getting hot. I assured this teacher that my son didn't know everything, and suggested that she might challenge him by having him do some independent research. She stared at me as if I had two heads.

- When my doctor's son was in second grade, he was in his school's gifted program. Since the program met at recess, he decided that he wanted to get out of it as soon as possible. However, he didn't want anyone to be disappointed in him. After thinking about this problem for a while, he had an idea. Every time he took a test or quiz, he answered all of the questions correctly and then figured out how many answers he needed to change to get a score that was in the 80s. He decided that the teacher would believe he was not smart enough to be in the program, but would not figure out what was going on because his test scores were still believable. He did the math and erased just the right number of correct answers each time. Of course, the teacher eventually caught on. When his mother found out what her son did, she sympathized with him. She agreed that having a gifted program during recess was a bad idea, and took him out of the program.

Above-level learners need to be included in the differentiation equation so they feel challenged and stimulated, too.

Anyone who has taught a classroom of youngsters for more than a few minutes understands the pressing need for differentiation. Few educators question this, but the looming question is how to differentiate instruction in a way that is manageable. Too often, practical suggestions for how this can be accomplished are lacking, and that is exactly what we will examine in this chapter. We will also look at strategies for easily managing classrooms where different students are pursuing the same goals in diverse ways.

Students come into our classrooms with different skill sets, learning styles, and diverse interests. According to Wendy Conklin (2006), there are three basic ways that teachers can differentiate instruction: through *content* (the resources and materials that are used for instruction), *process* (the way we ask students to make sense of what they are learning), and *product* (how students can share what they have learned).

You will notice some overlap between these three categories. It is possible to differentiate the content you provide, the process you use, and the product you require all at the same time. However, if this is the first time you are planning to formally differentiate your lessons, it is probably best to start with just one.

Each of these differentiation structures will be examined separately. In the appendices at the end of this book (Appendices E, F, and G, pages 165–169), you will find specific instructional techniques for differentiation using that structure.

Differentiation by Content

Just as the title of Richard Allington's article (2002) states: "You Can't Learn Much from Books You Can't Read." If students struggle to simply decode text, they cannot use their mental energy to understand the new information they read and make the necessary connections to it. Students at different skill levels need to have access to a variety of resources and materials that cover the same concepts but vary in readability, sophistication, and abstraction.

Meeting the needs of students who perform at different skill levels is not just about bringing the reading level up or down. Advanced students, who have demonstrated a mastery of the curriculum, need materials that go beyond the scope of what is regularly taught. They may profit from *compacting*, or spending less time with the regular curriculum, and more time with extension and enrichment opportunities. These students benefit from texts and other resources that are more sophisticated. You may want to give them texts that are more ambiguous (and thus open for interpretation) and that deal with concepts in interesting, novel, and sometimes controversial ways. Advanced students are often able to work with less direct teacher support. But just like any other students, you will need to meet with your advanced students on a regular basis to discuss what they are learning and to help them set and meet new goals.

On the other hand, students at lower skill levels require simpler and less ambiguous text. They may need text that is supported by illustrations, explanations, and other outside resources. These students often require ongoing support. Most likely, you will need to meet with them frequently to ensure that they are on track, to answer their questions, to encourage their efforts, and to help them if they become confused. English language learners need to have resources that provide extra context. They may need illustrations, picture dictionaries, translation materials, word banks, video clips, or people available who speak their native languages to make sense of what they are learning. For these students and for struggling native speakers, time may be needed to help fill in background information that is lacking.

As our students learn and grow, their needs continually change. Often, just by watching your students and listening to what they say, you can identify those who need immediate assistance and those who are ready to work independently. Sometimes, just a few words to a confused student or a short mini-lesson geared to a group with similar needs can make all of the difference.

There are two other things that you should take into consideration when differentiating by content: the interests and the learning styles (or learning preferences) of your students.

In schools, the curriculum is usually so packed with topics that we feel pressured to cover in the curriculum that we give our students little opportunity to choose what they are interested in studying. Although this might not be feasible all of the time, letting students make some choices about the texts that they read or the topics that they study leads to deeper engagement. It builds on their natural curiosity, their desire for autonomy, their need to feel respected, and their need to feel competent. Often, just letting students make choices will ensure greater determination, focus, and, ultimately, success. It also gives students the skills necessary for independent learning.

There are several ways to differentiate the content of instruction by student interest. Students may be given choices of books to read in a reader's workshop model or through literature circles (book groups). They can also be involved in independent research and choose the topic that they wish to study. If all students are studying the same topic, they can still be given a choice about which aspect of that topic they wish to investigate in depth.

The final consideration when it comes to differentiation by content is students' learning styles or preferences. Written text is not the only source of information. In this digital age, the definition of *text* itself has broadened. Different sources of information are more easily accessible than ever before. Students who learn best through art, music, movement, nature, or numeracy can now access pictures, video clips, statistical analyses, and songs that match their learning modalities. Many primary source materials have also become available to teachers through different educational publishers. These may include original letters, advertisements, posters, pictures, and more. New "texts" can now be easily integrated into the classroom through the technologies and educational resources that we have available today. (See the chart in Appendix E, pages 165–166, for a description of specific techniques for differentiating instruction by content. These techniques are based on the skill levels, interests, and learning styles of students. The chart also contains sample lessons so that you can see what these strategies might look like in a classroom setting.)

Differentiation by Process

Sometimes, even when we have great intentions and design special programs to differentiate instruction, we miss the mark. It is best to differentiate instruction as part of the regular classroom setting so that everyone can benefit. This is the root of differentiation by process.

The process of learning is the way that students make sense out of what they are studying. You can differentiate the process of learning for students by providing alternative activities that lead them to the same goals. You can target activities to students who perform at different skill levels, have different learning styles, interests, talents, or proclivities. There are many ways that this can be accomplished.

Differentiation of Process by Questioning

The simplest and most obvious way of differentiating the process of instruction is through questioning. The best-case scenario is when the questions come from those who are at the center of learning, namely, the students. If you encourage your students to ask lots of questions, and to explore the answers to those questions, it prevents them from becoming passive learners. It also gives them the message that their curiosity can lead to greater understanding. Celebrating student questions encourages them to seek help when they are confused. There are specific techniques for varying the complexity of the questions you ask, and some of these techniques will be detailed in the chart on differentiating by process (see Appendix F, pages 167–168).

Differentiation of Process by Assignments

There are several simple ways to differentiate the assignments that you give based on the different skill levels of your students. One way is to vary the complexity by either narrowing or broadening the task. For struggling students and for English language learners, you may narrow the scope of any assignment by limiting requirements. You may add context for students by providing additional resources such as video clips, illustrations, or diagrams. You may also break the assignment into manageable parts or provide additional activities to help fill in gaps in their background knowledge.

For advanced students, you may broaden the scope of any activity by providing additional open-ended questions or by giving them tasks that call for interpretation. You can also give assignments that require more complex and advanced thinking, or ask students to do independent research.

Two other ways to differentiate the process of instruction is to give students choices or to have them involved in inquiry-based learning. In choice-based learning, students decide which activities to complete based on their interests, preferences, or learning styles. In inquiry-based learning, students can explore materials and grapple with interesting and thought provoking questions to construct meaning in their own way.

(See the chart in Appendix F, pages 167–168, for some specific strategies for differentiation by process.)

Differentiation by Product

"The most important thing about curriculum differentiation is that it respects and responds to student differences."

—Jeanne Purcell and Deb Burns, 2004

Teachers can differentiate the products that students need to produce to demonstrate their mastery of new concepts. As with content and process, differentiation by product can be accomplished in several different ways.

The simplest way to differentiate by product is to give students a choice about how they want to demonstrate their understanding. If students have the opportunity to choose the type of product that they will produce, they are more likely to be invested in the work and be motivated to do a good job. They may also be able to use (2002) their natural interests and talents to make connections to the new material. There are many sources of alternative product ideas available to teachers from which students can choose. However, sometimes it is motivating for students themselves to come up with the type of project or presentation that they wish to do. If you choose to let your students do this, make sure that they know the criteria that will be used for evaluation, and that they have secured your approval, before they begin.

There are two important parameters involved when giving students any type of choice. The students must completely understand the goals of the instruction and they must understand how their efforts will be critiqued.

You can differentiate by product and still make adjustments based on the skill level of your students. You may give your below grade-level students and English language learners performance requirements that are narrower in scope and require more concrete thinking. You may require your above grade level students to demonstrate their thinking in more complex or advanced ways. If you choose to do this, just make sure that every student feels that they are doing something personally challenging and that they have the opportunity to share what they learned with the class. (See the chart in Appendix G, page 169, for some specific strategies regarding differentiating instruction by product.)

Conclusion

Students come into our classrooms with widely diverse backgrounds and abilities and every teacher understands the pressing need for targeting instruction to the different needs of their students. The more perplexing question is how to do this in a way that is manageable. Teachers can differentiate through the content (the resources and materials they use), process (how students make sense of information), and/or product (how students demonstrate their understanding). Fortunately, there are specific techniques that teachers can use to differentiate instruction both efficiently and effectively.

Reflection

1. Why is differentiating instruction necessary?

2. How can you plan for differentiated instruction using the Backwards Planning model in your classroom?

3. What are three specific ways that you can differentiate your instruction by content, by process, and/or by product? What would you need to do to organize this type of differentiation so that lessons run smoothly in your classroom?

4. How can you differentiate your questioning technique so that each student experiences the appropriate amount of challenge?

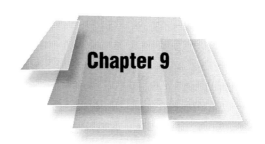

Chapter 9

Managing a Differentiated Classroom and Some Final Thoughts

> *"Differentiating is what I am doing when I feel great about my teaching. I planned for the differences, I took into account what the students were doing and what they showed me they knew. I thought out how I would match up what I would ask them to do, which resources I would use for whom, and what kinds of questions I would ask of different students."*
>
> —Jeanne Purcell and Deb Burns, 2004

Using the differentiation strategies described in the previous chapter will help you reach all of your students. However, running a student-centered classroom, where students are involved in lots of hands-on activities, requires strong management skills. Much of the time, you will be busy working with small groups or conferencing with individual students. In order to provide different types of instruction, you need to set up your classroom so that your students can work as independently as possible. You need to teach your students procedures that will enable them to become self-sufficient and successful. We will now examine some techniques to make differentiating instruction manageable.

Room Setup

It is important to set up your room in a way that allows for student engagement and exploration. If your desks are always in rows, and you are always in the front of the room, it is difficult for students to have a meaningful discussion or to work in small groups. If your room is large, it is best to have designated areas in which you can work with the entire class or with small groups. Even if your room is small, you can still have your students move the furniture so that they can work independently or with each other.

Resources

Your instructional materials should be easily accessible to you and the resources that your students need for learning need to be easily accessible to them. This means that you must organize materials so that your students can get (and return) what they need quickly and efficiently without interrupting you. Classroom book collections need to be arranged in ways that make it easy for students to find what they need. Materials for completing assignments (such as paper, markers, crayons, glue, scissors, or rulers) must be housed in places that students can reach. Here are some tips for organizing materials and resources in a differentiated classroom.

- Gather materials on different readability levels on the topics or subjects that you are teaching in advance. Many resources may be downloaded from the Internet, and school and local public libraries are great sources of information on different readability levels. Arrange these materials so that your students can easily get them when needed.

- If possible, gather illustrations, photographs, charts, graphs, video clips, picture dictionaries, thesauruses, and other resources that will help your English Language Learners and below grade-level students make sense of new material.

- Organize some of your classroom books and articles in different ways for easy access. Resources can be organized by topic, level, or genre. Use labeled baskets or bins for some of the resources so that students can flip through them easily.

Managing Materials

Students need to practice the procedures involved in getting, using, and returning materials correctly. You need to think about all of the different procedures that you want your students to follow for your room to flow smoothly. You need to explain the procedures one at a time, demonstrate them, and have students practice them until they become routine. Here are a few tips you might want to consider for distributing and collecting differentiated assignments. Many of the following ideas come from Wendy Conklin's *Applying Differentiated Strategies* (2009):

- Code your differentiated assignments with a symbol so that you can easily distinguish their levels. When you are handing out the sheets, stack them so that the most difficult ones are on the bottom, the average ones in the middle, and the easiest ones are on the top. Hold the leveled assignments between your fingers so that you can quickly distribute the correct assignment to each student.

- Write the names of the students on the differentiated sheets *before* handing them out to make the process more efficient.

- Prepare all materials for each activity that you are assigning in advance, and have them ready for easy distribution. For example, you may put the materials that specific groups of students will need in different boxes.

- Place differentiated activity bins in different locations of the room and direct students to pick up their work in the correct place. This avoids the problem of handing out different sheets to different students.

- Have a designated box (or boxes) for the collection of assignments.

Independent and Group Work

In order to manage groups of students who are working on different tasks, you will need to organize your time so that you gradually release the responsibility of learning to your students.

You begin by modeling whatever it is you want your students to accomplish, guide them as they begin to work independently or in small groups, give them adequate time for independent or group investigations, and have them share what they have learned. As students work, you will need to circulate around the classroom and conference with them to make sure that they are on task and productive and to help them set and achieve goals. You will need to train your students to help each other so that they do not have to depend on you for everything. Here are a few tips for managing differentiated group work:

- **Model all aspects of what you want your students to do.** Demonstrate how you use the strategies that you want them to use. Think out loud. Show students exactly how you want them to record their thinking as they work. Give them the chance to practice what you want them to do in front of you before having them work individually or in small groups. You may also teach, model, and role-play social skills such as making eye contact, taking turns, giving everyone air time, staying on task, being courteous when disagreeing, and helping each other.

- **Institute the policy, "Ask three, then me."** Explain to students that before they will get your assistance, you will expect them to tell you three ways they tried to find the answer on their own.

- **Review all rules of effective teamwork** *before* students begin their work.

- **Make sure that your directions are clear** and that everyone knows what is expected of them before having students go off on their own. You may ask students to repeat the directions. You will probably need to work more extensively with your English language learners and below-level students before having them try to do the work independently, with partners, or in small groups.

- **Seat students** who are studying the same topic or who are on a similar skill level **near each other** so that they can assist each other.

- If possible, have **English language learners work in groups** with others who are proficient in both English and in their native tongues, so that the English language learners can get timely assistance.

- **Make sure that all students have the materials** and resources that they need to complete the assignments successfully.

- **Circulate during group work** to help students solve problems as they arise.

- **Teach students how to help each other** in constructive ways. Provide structured opportunities for students to give and receive feedback from each other.

- **Have students reflect on the work that they are doing.** Ask them to talk about the strategies that they used that were the most useful to them. Have them critique their own learning and the learning of their groups. They may answer questions such as: What was easy for you (or your group) and why? What was difficult for you (or your group) and why? What was your role in the group task and how well did you perform? What might you (or your group) do to improve the quality of the work next time?

- **Have interesting and relevant anchor or structured activities ready** for individuals or groups of students who finish their assignments early. The content and quality of these activities is important. Piling on "busy work" is counterproductive, because mindless assignments hinder education. Also, students soon realize that if they are efficient and on task, their reward is they will get to do something repetitive and boring. Anchor activities must be both meaningful and enjoyable. They should extend the goals being sought.

Record Keeping

You need to keep track of the ongoing progress of your whole class, small groups of students, and individual students. You can do this in different ways. If you are using a traditional grading book, you will need to label what you are grading. You may also wish to color code individual versus group grades. If you are keeping anecdotal records, you may use a notebook with a designated area for each student and take quick notes on the progress you see, the concerns that you have, and ideas for meeting individual needs. You should also provide reflection sheets for students so that they can continually evaluate the quality of their individual work, as well as their group work.

Conclusion

Chinese philosopher Lao Tzu (604 BC – 531 BC) said, "A journey of a thousand miles begins with a single step." As a teacher, you have the power to touch the future. Through your knowledge of your subject, your understanding of effective instruction, your ability to manage your classroom, your responsiveness to the needs of your students, and your careful planning, you have the tools to open up the minds of the young people in your charge. You can pique your students' curiosity and provide the scaffolding they need to succeed. You can have a vital impact on their future lives. Talk about a life well spent!

Remember that this is a journey, and you are in it for the long haul, so it is important to be comfortable. If you are planning a unit using Backwards Planning principles for the first time, start small and collaborate with others, if possible. Start with content that you enjoy teaching and that you are passionate about. Use the differentiation techniques that meet your needs and are the easiest to manage. Don't worry about doing things perfectly. As you reflect on your practices and on the responsiveness of your students, you will always be able to make changes as you go.

There are many ways that you can use Backwards Planning principles effectively and efficiently. However, to teach your students for enduring understanding, keep the fundamentals in mind. Start with your end goals. Work backwards to determine what your students will need to do to prove to you that they "get it." Finally, focus on designing lessons that will enable your students to construct meaning.

If you stick to the process, you have a great shot at helping your students reach the goals that you are seeking. Along your journey, remember to keep track of your successes. The fact that you are willing to try new things to improve your craft already puts you in the highest echelon of your profession.

Now, enjoy your journey! What you do makes *all* the difference.

Reflection

1. Given whatever constraints you have, what do you think would be the optimal classroom set-up for you to differentiate instruction?

2. What are some ways that you can organize and manage resources in your classroom so that your students can work independently?

3. What systems can you put in place to best manage group work and keep track of individual and group progress? How will you communicate these ideas to your students? To administration? To parents?

Gradual Release of Responsibility Model

Effective teaching occurs when you gradually release the responsibility of learning to your students. This model comes from the work of Pearson and Gallagher (1983), and there are several phases involved:

Phase	Steps Involved
Modeling or Demonstration	• **Explain and model** the new concept, idea, or strategy that you are teaching to your students. **Think aloud** as you show your students exactly what will be expected of them in a 10–15 minute mini-lesson. Demonstrate how you use the procedures and strategies you would like them to use, how you want them to record their thinking, etc. • **Students listen and observe**, and they may participate in a limited way.
Guided Practice	• **Interact with your students** and guide them as they begin to gain independence by doing what you have demonstrated. Clarify, coach, react to students, and make suggestions as your students listen, respond, ask questions, collaborate with each other, and try out the new learning under your guidance.
Independent Practice	• **Release the responsibility of learning to your students.** Students need lots of time to practice, problem solve, self-correct, and work independently as they use new concepts and skills. • **Observe what your students are doing.** Conference with them, answer their questions, encourage them to think through problems, and clarify any misunderstandings they might have. • **Provide scaffolds or focused supports** for those students who struggle so that everyone can be successful. It's important for students to use materials and resources that are on the right level for them so that they do not get bored, frustrated, or discouraged. Remove scaffolds when they are no longer needed so that your students no longer depend on them.

Gradual Release of Responsibility Model *(cont.)*

Phase	Steps Involved
Application	• **Students apply their new learning to novel situations.** They should be self-directed and self-evaluative and may ask you for confirmation or clarification. • **Be responsive to your students.** Encourage and assist them as needed; help them navigate around stumbling blocks, and help them set new attainable goals.
Reflection and Sharing	• **Students reflect on what they are learning, discuss new concepts, and think about their progress.** Students react to the information they are learning and the usefulness of the strategies they are using. • **Give students continual feedback and provide opportunities for them to give feedback to each other.** This will help them become responsive to their own learning processes, understand their goals, become aware of their problems, and celebrate the progress they are making. • **Students become self-reflective and take control of their own learning.**

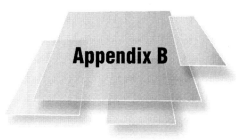

Appendix B

Backwards Planning At-a-Glance

Stage One: Identify Desired Results
What should my students know, understand, and be able to do? What is worthy of understanding? What enduring understandings are desired?

Content Standard(s)
What are the national, state, and/or local standards for the topic or subject you are teaching?

Big Idea(s) or Enduring Understanding(s)
List the big ideas or organizing principles of the topic. What are the universal concepts that have enduring relevance?

Essential or Guiding Question(s)
List three to five over-arching questions that will guide student inquiry. What questions will help students use their knowledge effectively over time?

Specific Understandings
List the specific understandings that will lead your students to the big ideas or essential goals of the unit of study. What specific understandings do you want your students to acquire around these big ideas? How will these general principles frame the factual information to build a conceptual understanding?

Possible Misunderstandings
List possible misunderstandings that could impede learning.

Student Objectives
List observable and measurable outcomes towards your goals that you can assess.

Learning Targets—Enabling Knowledge
List the facts, concepts, and principles that will help students form a conceptual framework around the unit's big ideas.

Learning Targets—Enabling Skills
List the procedures, strategies, and methods that your students must be able to use to perform effectively.

Culminating Activity
How will students demonstrate their achievement of the goals of instruction? How will they present their work? Who will be their authentic audience?

Stage Two: Determine the Assessment Evidence
Learning Targets and Assessment Evidence

List learning targets in the left-hand column. Specify what performance and written assessment evidence will be used to determine achievement of each of those learning targets in the right-hand column. Assessments may include products, written work, performance, or other evidence of understanding.

Stage Three: Plan Learning Experiences and Instruction
Activities
Make a rough time line or calendar of the benchmarks students must meet. Include the supporting activities that will prepare them to reach the instructional goals. (See Appendix D, page 164, for an example.)

Prerequisite Skills
Which foundational skills will require direct instruction and which lend themselves to student investigation? How will students apply what they have learned?

Materials
Are there any specific materials the unit will require?

Differentiation
How will you differentiate instruction to meet the needs of all students (by process, product, and content)? What materials, resources, and activities would be useful in differentiating instruction based on student needs, interests, and/or learning styles?

Planning Your Own Unit of Study

Topic: _____   **Grade Level:** _____

Length of Unit of Study: _____

Stage One: Identify Desired Results	
Content Standard(s):	
Big Idea(s) or Enduring Understanding(s):	**Essential or Guiding Question(s):**
Specific Understandings:	**Possible Misunderstandings:**
Student Objectives:	
Learning Targets—Enabling Knowledge:	**Learning Targets—Enabling Skills:**
Culminating Activity:	

Stage Two: Determine the Assessment Evidence	
Learning Targets: • _____ • _____	**Assessment Evidence:** • _____ • _____

Stage Three: Plan Learning Experiences and Instruction

Make a rough time line or calendar of the benchmarks students must meet and the supporting activities that will prepare students for the final goals.

Activities:	Prerequisite Skills:
• _____ • _____	• _____ • _____
Materials: • _____ • _____	**Differentiation:** • _____ • _____

Sample Unit Overview Grid for the Ecology Unit

	Day 1	Day 2	Day 3	Day 4	Day 5
Week of Nov. 1	Introduction to environmental balance and natural resources	Field trip to local watershed Discussion of findings	Discuss problems that need to be solved Group work: Brainstorm possible solutions to problems	Select community problem to solve Choose topics for research article based on this problem	Begin research process Work in pairs to determine questions to answer and research materials to use
Week of Nov. 8	Discussion of experimental design	Experiment on using resources in ways that are not sustainable	Experiment continued…	Report findings from experiment	Poster on renewable resources due
Week of Nov. 15	Send invitations for teach-in (culminating activity) Work on research article	Work on research article continued…	First draft of student research articles due Students meet in peer editing groups	Peer editing and review of articles continued…	Begin the revision and editing process of research articles
Week of Nov. 22	Final draft of articles due	Assemble magazine	Practice for presentation	Distribute magazine to teachers and community members	Culminating activity: Teach-in with community members

Strategies for Differentiation by Content

Differentiation Technique	Description
Tiered Instruction Using Leveled Text	**By skill level:** A variety of texts or other resources that include the same essential concepts, but are written in more or less complex ways. **By interest or learning style:** A choice of subjects or topics to explore, as well as the types of informational materials. *Note:* Materials that cover the same concepts but that are written on different readability levels should be available for all tiered lessons.
Independent Investigations	Students explore topics that are of particular interest to them and that will lead them to a specific learning goal. Teacher provides texts or other resources that pertain to these topics, or students conduct independent research.
Learning Contracts	Students sign individual agreements with teachers that specify how they intend to reach a specific learning goal. The contract stipulates what that student will learn and the assessments (assignments or presentations) that will serve as evidence of learning. *Note:* The contracts may also include behavioral expectations.
Book Choices Through Readers' Workshop	Students choose books to read with teacher guidance. The structure of the Reader's Workshop model includes modeling, guided practice, independent practice, and reflection and sharing. **Modeling:** The teacher introduces a reading strategy using a mini-lesson with a short text. **Guided practice:** Students practice the strategy as a group using the modeled text (under the direct guidance of the teacher). **Independent practice:** Students choose books (teachers ensure an appropriate reading level as needed). Students record their thinking. Teachers confer with students to check understanding and deepen thinking. **Reflection/sharing:** At the end of the session, students share what they have learned with their classmates.

Strategies for Differentiation by Content *(cont.)*

Differentiation Technique	Description
Book Choices Through Literature Circles (Book Groups)	Students choose the book (short story, or article) that they wish to read. They discuss the text with others who have read the same one. The structure of the lesson includes an introduction of the text, an opportunity for independent reading, meetings with book groups at specified intervals, and time for reflection and sharing.
	Introduction of the text: The teacher introduces several short stories or articles by reading the blurb or article abstract and passages from the text, which students take time to preview. Students make informed decisions about which text to choose based on the topic, the author's writing style, and the readability level. The teacher reviews student choices and forms book groups.
	Independent reading: Students read specified portions of the text independently and take notes with an explicit focus (set by the teacher or by group members).
	Meeting with book groups: Students who are reading the same text meet at regular intervals (after specific portions of the text have been completed). They discuss their observations and set goals for the next meeting.
	Reflection/sharing: When the reading is complete, each group presents what it discovered about the book, short story, or article.

Strategies for Differentiation by Process

Differentiated Technique	Description
Tiered Assignments	Students complete parallel tasks with similar goals. Assignments may vary in complexity, abstraction, and/or depth, but all are appropriately challenging. The teacher provides scaffolds, supports, and enrichment activities that different students need to complete the tasks successfully. All students work toward the same goals, but with a greater likelihood for success because the tasks are appropriately challenging.
Leveled Questioning (Using Bloom's Taxonomy)	Adjust questions based on the specific skill levels and abilities of different students. Match the appropriate level of questions to your students' knowledge and skill levels. Skills progress as follows: **Remembering (recognizing or recall):** Definitions and retelling (*who, what, where,* and *how*). **Understanding (comprehension):** Construction of meaning (*why, compare, explain, give examples, summarize*). **Applying (using knowledge to solve problems):** Use knowledge (*apply, demonstrate, implement, execute, solve, show*). **Analyzing (examining specific parts to come up with ideas and solutions):** Examine specific pieces of information, clues, or parts of a problem in order to reach conclusions, to devise solutions, or to develop new ideas. **Evaluating (judging the value of something based on supported evidence):** Appraise, judge, critique, and present the pros and cons of a subject or topic. **Creation (using what you know to create something new and different):** Think about what is learned, what is already known, and related or relevant experiences in order to create something new and different (*create, design, invent, devise, plan, develop, formulate, produce, generalize, combine, compose, modify,* or figure out "what if" scenarios).

Strategies for Differentiation by Process (cont.)

Differentiation Technique	Description
Leveled Questioning (Using Kaplan's Depth and Complexity Strategy)	Depth and complexity are interrelated and can be used to reinforce each other. Strategies that may be useful in guiding students to greater depths of knowledge and understanding include: looking for patterns, examining the rules, understanding the big ideas, and looking at the subject over time.
Leveled Questioning (Using Three-Story Intellect)	A simplified form of Bloom's Taxonomy that is based on how the brain works. There are three stages: gathering information, processing information for understanding, and using the information.
Choices (Based on Gardner's Multiple Intelligences)	A broad range of intelligence types account for human potential in children and adults, beyond traditional IQ. This theory states that every person possesses each type of intelligence but develops some more fully than others. Differentiate based on one of the seven intelligences, including: verbal/linguistic, logical/mathematical, bodily/kinesthetic, visual/spatial, interpersonal, intrapersonal, and musical/rhythmic. (Naturalistic intelligence was later added, and some consideration has been given to adding existential, moral, and/or spiritual intelligences.)
Inquiry-Based Learning, Problem Based Learning, and Creative Problem-Solving	Students' questions drive instruction. Students investigate and solve problems that they pose themselves and that are rooted in the real world. In *problem-based learning*, students work in small groups to seek solutions to authentic problems or to problems that mirror real-world situations. In *creative problem solving*, students develop their own independent and creative solutions to real-world problems. Creativity involves looking at problems in new ways, seeing things from multiple perspectives, and being tolerant of ambiguity.
Discovery Learning	Students use past experiences and existing knowledge to discover facts and relationships and to come to new truths about a topic or subject.

Appendix G

Strategies for Differentiation by Product

Differentiation Technique	Description
Menu of Options	The teacher determines different activities that will help students reach the desired goal. The tasks are of differing complexity, and are worth different scores, points, or grades. The teacher presents the options and students choose which to complete.
Choices Board	The teacher writes activity choices that lead to the instructional goals (skills, ideas, concepts, or generalizations) on index cards and posts them in random order on a chart. The cards should have symbols (or colors) to denote above-grade level, on-grade level, below-grade level, and English language learners. Based on their proficiency levels, students choose an appropriate number of activities. After completing the leveled activities successfully, students can complete a challenge activity from a higher-level card or create their own activity.
Differentiated Learning Stations or Centers	Hands-on activities are situated in special locations in the classroom (such as a computer or library center) that contain different types of resource materials for reading and writing assignments, learning games, listening activities, computer-based assignments, construction activities, dramatic play, exploration of manipulatives, academic contests, research activities, experiments, and more.

References Cited

Allington, R. 2002. You can't learn much from books you can't read. *Educational Leadership*, vol. 60:16–19.

Anderson, L. W., and D. R. Krathwohl. 2001. *A taxonomy for learning, teaching and assessing: A revision of Bloom's taxonomy of educational objectives*, complete edition. New York: Longman.

Baccellieri, P. 2010. *Professional learning communities: Using data in decision making to improve student learning.* Huntington Beach, CA: Shell Education.

Bernhardt, V. 2004. *Data analysis for continuous school improvement.* Larchmont, NY: Eye on Education, Inc.

Bransford, J. D., A. L. Brown, R. R. Cocking, and National Research Council. 1999. *How people learn brain, mind, experience, and school.* Washington, D.C.: National Academy Press.

Case, B., and S. Zucker. 2005. *Horizontal and vertical alignment.* Presented at the China–U.S. Conference on Alignment of Assessments and Instruction in Beijing, China.

Chan, W. 1963. *The way of Lao Tzu.* New York: Prentice-Hall.

Chase, C. I. 1999. *Contemporary assessment for educators.* New York: Addison-Wesley Longman.

Collins, A. 1996. Design issues for learning environments. In *International Perspectives on the Psychological Foundations of Technology-based Learning Environments.* 347–361. Mahwah, NJ: Lawrence Erlbaum Associates.

Conklin, W. 2006. *Instructional strategies for diverse learners.* Huntington Beach, CA: Shell Education.

_____. 2009. *Applying differentiated strategies: Teachers handbook for secondary.* Huntington Beach, CA: Shell Education.

Conklin, W. (H. Isecke, contributing author). 2010. *Differentiated strategies in mathematics.* Huntington Beach, CA: Shell Education.

Costa, Arthur L. 2007. *The school as a home for the mind: Creating mindful curriculum, instruction, and dialogue.* Thousand Oaks, CA: Corwin Press.

Culham, R. 2003. *6 + 1 traits of writing.* New York: Scholastic.

Diaz, D. P., and R. B. Cartnal. 1999. Students' learning styles in two classes: Online distance learning and equivalent on-campus. *College Teaching*, vol. 47.

Donelson, W. J., and R. W. Donelson. 2010. *Implementing response to intervention.* Huntington Beach, CA: Shell Education.

Duch, B. 1999. Problem-based learning. *Institute for Transforming Undergraduate Education: Problem-Based Learning at University of Delaware.* **http://www.udel.edu/pbl/**.

DuFour, R. 2004. Schools as learning communities. *Educational Leadership,* vol. 61:6–11.

Edina Minnesota Public Schools. 2009. Six traits of writing: Online writing lab for elementary students. *Edina Public Schools.* **http://www.edina.k12.mn.us/concord/teacherlinks/sixtraits/sixtraits.html.**

Elbow, P. 1998. *Writing without teachers.* New York, NY: Oxford University Press.

Ertmer, P. A., and T. J. Newby. 1996. The expert learner: Strategic, self-regulated, and reflective. *Instructional Science* 24: 1-24. Netherlands: Kluwer Academic Publishers

Fisch, K., and S. McLeod. 2007. *Did you know?/Shift happens* **http://www.youtube.com/watch?v=ljbI-363A2Q.**

Gardner, Howard. 1993. *Frames of mind: The theory of multiple intelligences.* New York: Basic Books.

Garrison, C., and M. Ehringhaus. n.d. Formative and summative assessments in the classroom. *National Middle School Association.* **http://www.nmsa.org/Publications/**

Glasser, W. 1992. Quality, trust, and redefining education. *Education Week,* May 13.

_____. William Glasser quotes. *ThinkExist.com.* **http://thinkexist. com/quotes/william_glasser/.**

Hardin, G. 1968. The tragedy of the commons. *Science.* 162 no. 3859 (December 13):1243–1248 **http://www. sciencemag.org/cgi/content/abstract/162/3859/1243.**

Harel, I., and S. Papert. 1991. *Constructionism.* Norwood, NJ: Ablex.

Harris, J. H., and L. G. Katz. 2000. *Young investigators: The project approach in the early years.* New York: Teachers College Press.

Harvey, S. 1998. *Nonfiction matters.* Portland, ME: Stenhouse.

Hudson, B. 2004. Active thoughts about passive learning. *Musings: Pedagogically speaking—5531 rhetorical ways to skin a class.* **http://blog.lib.umn.edu/arrig002/5531/005721.html.**

Jacobs, H. H. 1997. *Mapping the big picture, integrating curriculum and assessment K-12.* 26, 67, 30, 31. Virginia: Association for Supervision and Curriculum Development.

Jensen, E. 1998. *Teaching with the brain in mind.* Alexandria, VA: Association for Supervision and Curriculum Development.

Kaplan, S. 2001. *Lessons from the middle: High-end learning for middle-school students.* Waco, TX: Texas Association for the Gifted and Talented.

Lavoie, R. 2005. Fairness: To each according to his needs. RickLavoie.com. **http://www.ricklavoie.com/fairnessart.html.**

Leipzig, D. H. 2000. Differentiated classroom structures for literacy instruction. Adapted from: Differentiated or just different? *Reading Rockets.* **http://www.readingrockets.org/ article/264**

Lerman, L. 2003. *The critical response process—A method for getting useful feedback on anything you make, from dance to dessert.* Takoma Park, MD: Liz Lerman Dance Exchange.

Levack, W. 2007. Smart goals: Who created this acronym? *Goal Setting and Achievement.* University of Otago, Wellington, New Zealand. **http://www.effexis2.com/forum/showthread. php?t=1546**

Marzano, R. J. 1992. *A Different kind of classroom: Teaching with dimensions of learning.* Alexandria, VA: Association for Supervision and Curriculum Development.

Marzano, R. J., D. J. Pickering, and J. E. Pollock. 2001. *Classroom instruction that works: Research-based strategies for increasing student achievement.* Alexandria, VA: Association for Supervision and Curriculum Development.

McKenzie, J. 1998. The WIRED classroom, creating technology enhanced student-centered learning environments. *From Now On, The Educational Technology Journal.* **http://www.FNO.org**. March, vol. 7: no. 6.

McPherson, F. 2001. About expert knowledge. *Mempowered.* **http://www.memory-key.com/improving**

McTighe, J., and E. Seif. 2003. *A summary of underlying theory and research base for Understanding by Design.* Unpublished manuscript.

Mertler, C. A. 2001. Using performance assessment in your classroom. *Unpublished manuscript.* Ohio: Bowling Green State University.

Mobus, G. 2007. From whence cometh wisdom? *George Mobus' Research Interests.* **http://faculty.washington.edu/gmobus/ research.html.**

Mueller, J. 2008. What is authentic assessment? *Principles of Authentic Assessment.* North Central College. Naperville, Illinois. **http://principlesauthenticassessment.blogspot.com/**

Nikitina, A. 2001. *Educational assessment of students.* (3rd ed.) Uppersaddle River, NJ: Prentice Hall, Inc.

———. 2010. Smart goal setting: A surefire way to achieve your goals. *Goal Setting Guide.* **http://www.goal-setting-guide.com/smart-goals.html.**

Office of Communications and Public Liaison National Institute of Neurological Disorders and Stroke. 2005. *The life and death of a neuron.* Bethesda, MD: National Institutes of Health.

Papert, S. 2009. Project-based learning: What works in public education. *Edutopia.* The George Lucas Educational Foundation. **http://www.edutopia.org/seymour-papert-project-based-learning.**

Pearson, P. D., and M. C. Gallagher. 1983. The instruction of reading comprehension. *Contemporary Educational Psychology,* vol. 8:317–344.

Perfetto, G. A., J. D. Bransford, and J. J. Franks. 1983. Constraints on access in a problem solving context. *Memory and Cognition*, vol. 11:24–31.

Perl, S. 1995. *Landmark essays on writing process.* Davis, CA: Psychology Press.

Perry, B. 2000. How the brain learns best. *Instructor magazine.* November/December.

Peters, T. 1994. *The pursuit of wow! Every person's guide to topsy-turvy times.* New York: Vintage Books.

Purcell, J., and D. Burns. 2004. Capturing the essence of curriculum differentiation. *The Trillium.* ASCD. Ontario.

Schacter, D. L. 1992. Understanding implicit memory. *American Psychologist,* vol. *47:559–569.*

Shillinger, R. n.d. *Contemporary Educational Psychology.* **http://schillingereducationalconsultants.com.**

Simon, H. A. 1996. *Observations on the sciences of science learning.* Paper prepared for the Committee on Developments in the Science of Learning for the Sciences of Science Learning: An Interdisciplinary Discussion. Department of Psychology, Carnegie Mellon University.

Smith, M. K. 2002, 2008. Howard Gardner and multiple intelligences. *The Encyclopedia of Informal Education.* **http://www.infed.org/thinkers/gardner.htm.**

Sprenger, M. 2002. *Becoming a wiz at brain-based teaching: How to make every year your best year.* Thousand Oaks, CA: Corwin Press.

_____. 2008. *The Developing brain: Birth to age eight.* Thousand Oaks, CA: Corwin Press.

Stiggins, R. J., and Valencia, S. 1997. *What are the different forms of authentic assessment?* Orlando, Florida: Houghton Mifflin Company. **http://www.eduplace.com/rdg/res/litass/forms.html.**

Thomas, J. W. 2000. A review of research on project-based learning. *Buck Institute for Education: Project-based learning for the 21st century.* Novato, CA: Buck Institute for Education. **http://www.bie.or/index.php/site/RE/pbi_Research.29**

Tileston, D. W. 2004. *What every teacher should know about instructional planning.* Thousand Oaks, CA: Corwin Press.

_____. 2003. *What every teacher should know about learning, memory, and the brain.* Thousand Oaks, CA: Corwin Press.

Tomlinson, C. A. 1995. *How to differentiate instruction in mixed-ability classrooms.* Alexandria, VA: Association for Supervision and Curriculum Development.

Tomlinson, C. A., and J. McTighe. 2006. *Integrating differentiated instruction and understanding by design.* Alexandria, VA: Association for Supervision and Curriculum Development.

Wiggins. G. n.d. Big ideas—Exploring the essential questions of
education. *Big Ideas: An Authentic Education e-Journal.*
http://www.authenticeducation.org/bigideas

Wiggins, G. 2006. UbD in a Nutshell.pdf.
**http://74.125.47.132/search?q=cache:YLnPElcCt9kJ:ubd2
1c.wikispaces.com/file/view/UbD_nutshell.pdf+UbD+in+a
+Nutshellandcd=1andh1=enandct=clnkandgl=usandclient=f
irefox-a.**

Wiggins, G., and J. McTighe. 1998. *Understanding by design.*
Alexandria, VA: Association for Supervision and Curriculum
Development.

———. 2005. *Understanding by design: Expanded 2nd edition.*
Alexandria, VA: Association for Supervision and Curriculum
Development.

Wong, H., and R. Wong. 1998, 2001. *The first days of school: How
to be an effective teacher.* Mountainview, CA: Harry K. Wong
Publications.

Wormeli, R. 2007. *Differentiation: From planning to practice,
grades 6–12.* Portland, ME: Stenhouse.

alignment. The coordination of curriculum and instruction, both on a single grade level and from one grade level to the next, to ensure that students are efficiently and effectively taught the necessary skills and information to meet standards. *Horizontal alignment* (within a specific grade level) ensures that there is a consistency in what is taught in any single grade level across classrooms and schools. *Vertical alignment* (from one grade level to the next) ensures that there are no gaps or repeated information in the curriculum from one grade level to the next.

assessment. The process of measuring or evaluating students' knowledge, skills, understanding, performance, attitudes, and/or beliefs. Assessments can be formal or informal. There are many different types of assessments including: formative, summative, authentic, traditional, performance-based, screening, diagnostic, anecdotal, and progress-monitoring.

authentic assignments/assessments. Tasks that require students to demonstrate that they can use their knowledge and skills to solve problems that have value beyond the classroom and are rooted in real-world challenges. Students are especially motivated when they feel that the results of their work can benefit their communities.

automaticity. Performing a task or operation with speed, understanding, and accuracy. In order to be able to do tasks with automaticity, such as decode words based on sound-letter correspondence, students must have sufficient practice to internalize procedures so that they can perform them easily and accurately. This allows students to free their minds to think about the meaning of text.

Backwards Planning (or *Understanding by Design*). Planning with the end goal in mind. First, determine the desired results of instruction (what enduring understandings the students will develop because of what they are learning). Then, develop the essential or guiding questions that will guide student inquiry. Next, decide on the specific factual and procedural learning targets that will lead to the desired results. Then, delineate how students will demonstrate their understandings, skills, and knowledge. Finally, plan the day-to-day activities that will lead students to the final goals of instruction.

benchmark. A standard that delineates what a student should know and be able to do at a particular time or at a particular grade level; a standard for measuring performance.

big ideas. The underlying concepts, theories, principles, or themes that can be used as a framework to help the learner make sense of a subject or topic.

Bloom's Taxonomy. A list created by Benjamin Bloom that organizes learning into categories, from the most basic to the most complex. Categories include: remembering, understanding, applying, analyzing, evaluating, and creating.

choices board. A strategy for differentiating instruction by providing students with choices. The teacher writes leveled activity choices that lead to specific instructional goals on index cards and posts them in random order on a chart. These cards usually have symbols or colors that denote their level of difficulty. Students choose a designated number of activities from the appropriately leveled cards.

compacting curriculum. For advanced students or those who have already achieved mastery, spending less time with the regular curriculum, and more time with extension and enrichment opportunities.

conceptual framework. An organizing principle (or theory) about a topic around which a person connects information and constructs meaning. For example, in studying economics, a conceptual framework might be that the cost of an item depends on supply versus demand.

conditionalized knowledge. Knowledge that can be used in different situations or under different conditions. Much of what is taught in school leads to inert knowledge. When knowledge is inert, students can use it only to solve the specific problems which they are given in school, but cannot transfer their knowledge in new contexts. In order to help students attain conditionalized knowledge, teachers should explain (and show) students where, when, and how they can apply new knowledge in new contexts and give students opportunities to practice.

constructivist learning. An active way for students to make sense of what they are learning. Students make meaning from their investigations rather than passively receive information from others. Understanding increases when students actively use what they know to explore, negotiate, interpret, create ideas, or investigate solutions to problems.

data. Information. In data based educational decisions, the educator goes through the process of collecting, analyzing, and interpreting data about students in order to make instructional decisions and create educational plans. The data may include information on students' achievement levels, attendance records, observation of work habits, surveys on attitudes, interests, and learning styles, etc. Data can be gleaned from formal or informal assessments, report card grades, anecdotal reports, observations, portfolios, surveys, or interviews.

declarative objectives or knowledge learning targets. The critical facts and information that teachers want students to know as a result of instruction, including the dates, names, events, steps, formulas, and vocabulary necessary to understand a topic. Teachers can assist students in remembering and using these disconnected facts by activating the students' background knowledge, helping them make personal connections to the new material, providing multisensory activities to activate their different memory systems, and having students reflect on what they are learning.

diagnostic assessments. Testing instruments usually administered by a trained professional to students who are struggling when the reasons for lack of normal progress are not apparent. Diagnostic assessments are designed to provide detailed information about the specific source and nature of the deficits of students who are not progressing.

differentiation. Targeting instruction to meet the diverse needs of a population of students at different skill levels, with different learning styles, and/or with different interests within a single classroom. Through carefully structured lessons, techniques, and assignments, teachers may differentiate the content (what is taught), the process (how the students learn), and/or the product (what students are expected to produce).

enduring understanding. Students mull over interesting, big ideas and construct their own meanings about the underlying concepts that define a topic. Students learn how to apply their knowledge in new situations and use what they know to solve real problems.

essential or guiding questions. Questions at the heart of a unit of study that are open-ended, thought provoking, and help provide a framework for understanding a specific topic or subject. In order to be essential, the questions must foster the disciplined inquiry, investigation, and critical thinking that will lead to a deep understanding of the big ideas of the topic or subject.

evaluation checklist. A list of criteria for successfully completing a written or performance assignment or assessment.

facets of understanding. Six ways that students can demonstrate understanding. This includes the ability to explain, to interpret, to apply, to present new perspectives, to empathize, and to demonstrate self-knowledge.

formative assessment. Formal or anecdotal measurements used to gather data about student achievement in order to inform future instruction and to target it to student needs.

Gradual Release of Responsibility Model. An instructional approach developed by Pearson and Gallagher (1993). The responsibility for understanding and using new information shifts progressively over time from teacher-led instruction to student independence. The general steps include teacher demonstration, guided practice, independent practice, application, reflection, and sharing.

habits of mind. The values, attitudes, motivational levels, and skills people have that directly affect how they approach learning.

independent investigations. Structured opportunities for students to explore topics that are of particular interest to them and will lead them to specific learning goals. Texts and/or other resources that pertain to these topics may be provided by the teacher or may be researched by the students.

inert knowledge. Knowledge that cannot be transferred from one situation to another.

inquiry-based learning. An educational approach that is driven by a learner's questions rather than by a teacher's lessons. Students investigate and solve problems that they are curious about and that are rooted in the real world. In *problem-based learning*, students work in small groups to seek solutions to authentic problems or problems that mirror real-world situations. They brainstorm the different aspects of the problem, investigate it, find appropriate learning resources, and figure out how to solve it. In *creative problem-solving*, students develop their own independent and creative solutions to real-world problems by looking at problems in new ways and seeing things from multiple perspectives. In *discovery learning*, students ask questions. They explore and gather data, grapple with uncertainties, examine controversies, test hypotheses, and perform experiments to come to an understanding of the general concepts, big ideas, or governing principles involved in a subject or topic.

intervention strategies. Specific instructional techniques used to help students who are struggling with particular aspects of the curriculum.

Kaplan's Depth and Complexity Model. Shows the interrelated nature of depth and complexity and how they can be used to reinforce each other. Kaplan describes eight strategies to guide students to greater depths of knowledge and understanding from vocabulary development to the search for details, patterns, trends, unanswered questions, governing rules, ethics, and finally to the big ideas of the topic or subject. Kaplan also delineates three strategies for guiding students to greater complexity by studying the topic over time, examining it from multiple perspectives, and studying it via its interrelated disciplines. When you differentiate instruction using Kaplan's strategies, you adjust your questions/assignments based on the depth and/or complexity of the topic that your students are ready to investigate and answer.

learning centers or stations. Hands-on activities that are either location-based or housed in portable folders or bins. They may contain reading and writing assignments, learning games, listening activities, computer based assignments, construction activities, dramatic play, exploration of manipulatives, academic contests, experiments, etc. that lead students to specified goals. Students may choose which centers they would like to complete or rotate through all centers. Different students may be asked to produce products that require different levels of skill, sophistication, or complexity.

learning contracts. Teacher and students work together to delineate the student's individualized learning goal, how it will be achieved, the time frame, and the assessments, assignments, or performances that will prove that the goal(s) have been attained. Learning contracts may also include behavioral expectations for success.

learning styles. A person's preferred method of learning. Methods include: listening to information, reading about information, problem solving, constructing projects, working alone, or working in groups. Learning Style Inventories pose questions to students to determine their personal preferences for learning. These inventories are helpful for teachers in planning small group or individual instruction.

learning targets. What teachers want their students to know and be able to do as a result of the instruction provided.

literature circles or book groups. Students have the opportunity to choose a book (short story, article, etc.) that they want to read from several options, and they discuss the text at intervals with other students who are reading the same thing. Normally, students take notes that focus on their personal responses to the text. The text used may be fiction or nonfiction.

menu of options. A method of differentiating instruction. The teacher determines different activities that will help students reach the desired goal(s) of instruction and gives students the opportunity to choose the one(s) to complete.

metacognition. Self-reflection on one's learning. The ability to analyze and understand one's own learning processes and adapt strategies when learning is not successful. Metacognition is about an individual taking responsibility for his or her own learning, and it is critical for both understanding and applying new information effectively.

Multiple Intelligences. The theory that traditional IQ testing is far too limited in scope because there is a broad range of types of intelligences that account for human potential in children and adults. Developed by Dr. Howard Gardner (1983), differentiation by Multiple Intelligences is one way of targeting lessons to student's learning preferences. Gardner originally identified seven intelligences: verbal/linguistic, logical/mathematical, bodily/kinesthetic, visual/spatial, interpersonal, intrapersonal, and musical/rhythmic. Naturalistic intelligence was added later, and Gardner has also given consideration to adding existential and/or moral/spiritual intelligences to the list. The theory is that every person possesses each type of intelligence but develops some more fully than others.

outcome measures. The large-scale assessments that are usually mandated by the government or by school districts. They enable educators to determine the success of individual students, grade levels, subject areas, and/or instructional programs. Outcome assessments may be either norm-referenced or criterion-referenced. Norm-referenced tests compare achievements of students nationally by age or grade level. Criterion-referenced tests measure students' knowledge of grade appropriate content or skills.

pedagogical content knowledge. The information it takes to effectively teach a specific topic or subject. This includes knowledge about the information and skills students must have to understand the central concepts of a topic, typical difficulties students might encounter as they learn the topic, and specific strategies that will help students who are struggling with particular aspects of the content to succeed.

performance assessments. Assessments that require students to demonstrate the skills they have and what they can do. Students may be asked to complete an exercise, activity, or assignment that requires solving a problem, performing a task or experiment, participating in a performance or debate, or applying their knowledge in new situations.

prerequisite knowledge and skills. The background skills, information, concepts, and understandings that students must have before they can learn the new information or skills being presented.

procedural objectives or procedural learning targets. The skills that teachers want students to demonstrate (or what they want students to be able to do) as a result of instruction. This includes the steps, strategies, and processes necessary to perform different operations. Teachers can help students acquire procedural knowledge by explaining the connection between new procedures and previously learned ones, modeling new procedures, and giving students the opportunity to practice them. Teachers can help students shape procedures to make them their own, show students how procedures can be applied in different contexts, and give students opportunities to practice. Teachers can also have students reflect on the processes they use and note the changes that they make to become more efficient in using them.

progress monitoring. Assessments help the teacher determine whether students are learning what is being taught and whether the intervention strategies for struggling students are effective.

project- or problem-based learning. Instruction that is planned around student investigation and inquiry. Students must either complete an open-ended project or solve a complex problem that requires them to construct meaning and make connections about the critical ideas of a topic or subject from the work they do. An example of this might be for students to learn about how animals and plants depend on each other by creating a biosphere.

readers' workshop. An instructional model that combines explicit instruction on reading strategies with opportunities for independent reading and analyzing books at appropriate levels. Readers' workshop follows the Gradual Release of Responsibility Model in that it moves from direct teacher demonstration to student independence, through a series of steps, including modeling, guided practice, independent practice, and reflection and sharing. Students have the opportunity to choose individual books that are on the appropriate level for their independent work.

rubrics. Rating scales or guides used to evaluate student performances and products. *Analytic rubrics* outline all of the criteria used to evaluate the level of success of students on every aspect of the assignment or assessment. Descriptors explain the evaluation system for each criterion (such as what constitutes a beginning, developing, accomplished, and exemplary level). *Holistic rubrics* only delineate the criteria for evaluating student performance or products as a whole. Holistic rubrics are most useful when the emphasis is on a strong completed performance or product and weakness in one area isn't important.

scaffolds. Focused supports designed to help students who struggle with different aspects of the curriculum.

screening assessments. Instruments (usually administered at the beginning of a unit or school year) used to identify which students are on or above grade level and which ones require additional support to succeed.

shaping. Internalizing a set of procedures in order to make it one's own. It is one of the processes required for procedures to be stored in long term memory. Shaping requires the learner's involvement in the process. The learner generally begins with a basic model or set of procedures for how to accomplish a particular task. The learner then works through problems and makes changes in how the procedures are applied to make the process more effective, efficient, and workable for him or her.

simulation. The representation of a situation, behavior, or process using a scenario that is analogous to it. Students are asked to respond to the simulation to determine their understanding of the concepts involved and their ability to apply their knowledge. For example, high school biology students may be given a scenario about fish suddenly dying in a local pond that includes data on weather conditions, sewage problems, etc. and be asked to figure out how to solve this problem.

Six + 1 Traits of Writing. Criteria for evaluating student writing that includes: ideas, organization, voice, sentence fluency, word choice, conventions, and presentation.

SMART Goals. A mnemonic device that can be used for creating powerful goals. The letters stand for **S**pecific, **M**easurable, **A**ttainable, **R**ealistic, and **T**ime-bound.

standards. The detailed criteria that describe what students are expected to learn and be able to do by different grade levels. *Content* standards detail these expectations by subject area. *Performance* standards specify ways students must demonstrate that the content standards have been met.

strategic approach to problem solving. The specific strategies people use to approach new problems. These include using algorithms (a specific set of steps), tactics (general rules), or strategies (universal concepts) to solve a problem.

student-centered learning. Students are active participants and take a responsible role in their own education. The teacher structures the learning environment based on the needs, abilities, interests, and preferred learning styles of his or her students. The teacher then acts primarily as a facilitator while students are involved in active investigations.

summative assessments. Measures used to determine what students have learned because of instruction. They are used to reveal the results of instruction. They may be in written form, performance-based, project-based, or problem-based. Examples include federal, state, or district assessments, culminating presentations, unit tests, midterms, or final exams.

Three-Story Intellect. A simplified form of Bloom's Taxonomy. It has three stages: gathering information, processing information for understanding, and using the information. Questions and assignments based on Three-Story Intellect can be adjusted to the students' readiness levels.

tiered assignments. A method for differentiating instruction in which the teacher gives different students parallel tasks with similar goals, but that vary in complexity, abstractness, and depth. The teacher then provides the scaffolds, supports, or enrichment activities that different students need to complete tasks successfully.

traditional assessments. Generally, written tests that call for convergent (or specifically correct) answers.

transfer of knowledge. The ability to apply what a person has learned in one context to a novel situation or a new context. Teachers can help students transfer knowledge by explaining and showing students how the new information can be applied in different situations and giving students time to practice doing this and reflecting on the connections that they are making.

Websites

6 Traits of Writing. Edina Public Schools.
http://www.edina.k12.mn.us/concord/teacherlinks/ sixtraits/sixtraits.html

Archives of Information on Priorities of Previous Administrations, 2001–2009. U.S. Department of Education. **http://www.ed.gov/about/overview/mission/archived- priorities.html.**

Big Ideas: An Authentic Education e-Journal. Authentic Education. **http://www.authenticeducation.org/bigideas/article. lasso?artId=108**

Designing Scoring Rubrics for Your Classroom. Practical Assessment, Research & Evaluation. **http://pareonline.net/getvn.asp?v=7&n=25**

Educational Standards. Mid-continent Research for Education and Learning **http://www.mcrel.org/compendium/topicsDetail. asp?topicsID=69&subjectID=2**

Essential Questions. Greenville, MI Public School System. **http://www.greenville.k12.sc.us/League/esques.html.**

Genesee Community Charter School Curriculum. Genesee Community Charter School at the Rochester Museum and Science Center. **http://www.gccschool.org/about.**

Motivational and Inspirational Quotes About Education. Motivational and Inspirational Corner...America's System for Success.
http://www.motivational-inspirational-corner.com/ getquote.html?startrow=11andcategoryid=228.

Quotes on Education. Donald Simanek's Pages.
http://www.lhup.edu/~dsimanek/eduquote.htm.

SMART Goal Setting: A Surefire Way To Achieve Your Goals. Goal Setting Guide.
http://www.goal-setting-guide.com/smart-goals.html

A Review of Research on Problem Based Learning. Buck Institute for Education.
http://www.bie.org/index.php/site/RE/pbl_research/29

UbD Research. TeacherLingo.
http://teacherlingo.com/blogs/weteachteachers/ archive/2008/03/04/ubd-research.aspx

What Are the Different Forms of Authentic Assessment? Education Place.
http://www.eduplace.com/rdg/res/litass/forms.html

What is Authentic Assessment? Authentic Assessment Toolbox.
http://jonathan.mueller.faculty.noctrl.edu/toolbox/whatisit. htm